SEED OF SOUTH SUDAN

SEED OF SOUTH SUDAN

Memoir of a "Lost Boy" Refugee

Majok Marier *and*
Estelle Ford-Williamson

McFarland & Company, Inc., Publishers
Jefferson, North Carolina

LIBRARY OF CONGRESS CATALOGUING-IN-PUBLICATION DATA

Marier, Majok, 1980–
    Seed of South Sudan : memoir of a "lost boy" refugee / Majok
Marier and Estelle Ford-Williamson.
        p.   cm.
    Includes bibliographical references and index.

    ISBN 978-0-7864-7428-8 (softcover : acid free paper) ∞
    ISBN 978-1-4766-1497-7 (ebook)

    1. Marier, Majok, 1980–   2. Sudan—History—Civil war,
1983–2005—Personal narratives.   3. Refugee children—Sudan—
Biography.   4. Dinka (African people)—Biography.   5. Sudan—
History—Civil War, 1983–2005—Children.   6. Sudan—History—
Civil War, 1983–2005—Refugees.   7. South Sudan—Biography.
8. South Sudan—Social conditions.   I. Ford-Williamson, Estelle.
II. Title.
DT157.672.M37 2014
962.404'2092—dc23
[B]   2014010548

BRITISH LIBRARY CATALOGUING DATA ARE AVAILABLE

On the cover: Majok Marier standing amid sorghum grain near Pulkar,
South Sudan. Plants were sustenance on much of the journey.

Printed in the United States of America

*McFarland & Company, Inc., Publishers
    Box 611, Jefferson, North Carolina 28640
    www.mcfarlandpub.com*

To the many refugees who died fleeing along
the paths and in the camps where we lived
in Ethiopia, Sudan, and Kenya and to those
who continue to suffer in conflicts in Africa.

Table of Contents

Acknowledgments

I wish to thank those who helped me on my African journey:

Yar Chol Gueny, my mother; Alek Chol Gueny, my aunt; Ajok Mabor Malek, my wife.

Dut Machoul Beny, my uncle on the journey; Kau Riak; Akec Rang; Mading Amerdit; Kolnyin Nak Goljok; Chol Dhukpou Welken; Chol Wang Gar; Chier Malual Mayom; Mangar Maker Anyar; Langudi Poundak Reec; Laat Poundak Reec; Garang Ngong Malok; Bol Maliet Kumo; Chol Bayok Yiak; Laat Deng Reec; Mading Cheny Malok; Matur Riak; Matur Chol Makerlit; Ayat Deng Ayat; Agar Matak Awur; Majur Akol Acipia; Nyier Malek Nyach; Mapuor Mabor Pur; Makuol Akuei; Amal Madol Athieu; Manyang Mawut.

Mapour Majok Daung; Ngor Kur Mayol; Bol Deng Bol; Thiik Ayai.

Ater Akec Malek; Toul Ayat Mabil; Mabor Kau Akec; Daung Deng; Makuei Jok; Nypen Abbas Tong, Lost Girl.

Atak Juac; Akec Awolich; Matoc Kout; Madong Mading Ater; Mayom Maker; Malual Marier Maliet, my eldest brother; Abol Marier Maliet, my brother; Lela Marier Maliet, my sister; Mading Arialgu Maliet; Achol Makoi; Maker Amala Maliet, my cousin (father's brother's son) ; Nyakor Manyang Mager, cousin's daughter; Mabak Machar; Mamer Tur; Mou Malong; Yai Malek; Mangar Ayii; Laat Mathou; Awan Magal Ater; Marik Ngang Marik; Deng Akoon Deng King; Makoi Cithol Kotjok; Malek Cithol Kotjok; Juac Gor; Bishop Yel Nhial; Father Madol Akot; Father Mathiang Machol; Lual Deng Majok; Chier Arop; Chol Machol.

And those who have especially helped me in America:

Mama Gini Eagen; Father Greg Kenny, CMF; Father Jim Curran, CMF; Father Jose Kochuparampil, CMF; Janis Sundquist; Helen M. Coelho; Ann Mahoney; Jennifer Moore; Jennifer Mann; Judy Maves; Bill Snodgrass; Elizabeth Crosby; Mary T. Steele; Patricia Shafer; Suzy Blough; Cyndie Heiskell; Mustafa Noor; Lutheran Services of Georgia; Corpus Christi Catholic Church, Stone Mountain, GA; Mothering Across Continents.

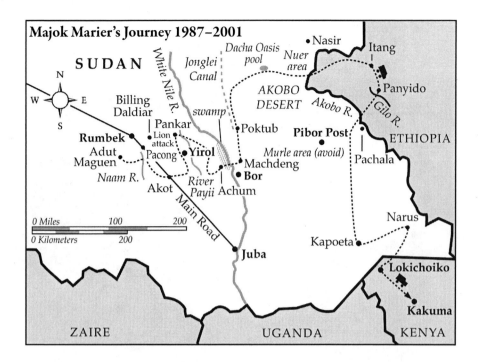

Majok Marier's Journey 1987–2001

xi

Nation of South Sudan, created July 9, 2011

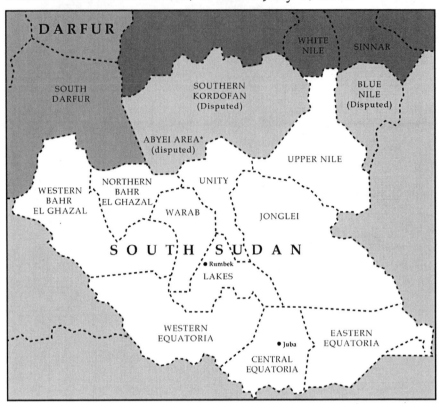

Preface

Western journalists in the bush country of southern Sudan in the 1980s reported seeing long lines of young boys walking in groups, sometimes very large groups. Overcoming language barriers, they asked the boys who they were. Piecing information together, the journalists learned they were boys whose villages had been burned by the Sudanese Army, and they were on the way to safety in Ethiopia. Aid workers eventually found them gathered where they'd been told to go—in refugee camps, or later, just in large fields that could accommodate the huge numbers where aid workers would then set up a camp. They were skeletons, only skin and bones, and when they arrived in one newly created camp, Panyido, they began dying of exhaustion, hunger, and disease.

Eventually there were tens of thousands in Panyido Refugee Camp. And then that one collapsed in 1991 during a rebellion in Ethiopia that toppled the Communist dictator. So they were forced on the paths again, to other camps.

Before events in Somalia, Rwanda, and even Darfur—suffering and death on an unimagined scale—southern Sudan was embroiled in a civil war the tragedy and scope of which the world was only learning. In 2000 and 2001, refugees from Sudan began arriving in U.S., Australian, and Canadian cities and towns. They'd acquired the name the Lost Boys of Sudan, after the orphan boys who followed the fictional Peter Pan in J.M. Barrie's play. National and local media in Chicago, Atlanta, Los Angeles, New York, Boston, Nashville, Kansas City, Phoenix, Jackson, Mississippi, and many others wrote articles and produced news stories on these men, and some women, who'd come to live in their midst. Now, 13 years after

1

their arrival, the civil war that cast them onto uncertain paths, the longest civil war in African history, has been settled. These men, and the many fewer women who came, can now carry on in their new lives.

This book tells the story of these young people through the eyes of a young Dinka man who was seven when the Sudanese Army attacked his village and he fled east to find safety. Majok Marier is now 33, and his story is told to share the day-by-day experience of his survival story and to bring readers up-to-date on his life and on those of others he met along the way. The account of Stephen Chol Bayok is also included, along with the stories of some of the many people who helped these young men in a world so far from their experience that they continue to be in wonder.

In addition to first-hand accounts, other resources, including news accounts and books on the conflict in Sudan have been consulted to provide understanding about this particular country and its culture, especially the customs and traditions of the Agar Dinka, and how Western, European and African nations have figured in the events that brought the men here. Majok's account is shown in Roman text, while text written by the co-author (as well as a short contribution by Stephen Chol Bayok) is in italics. In addition, sections providing information about people who helped the young men and historical background on South Sudan are indicated in the Table of Contents.

This is the first major work by a Lost Boy since the new nation of South Sudan was formed in 2011, and it includes recent news of several of the Lost Boys and their current lives. The scars of the journey are still there, but there are many lessons for people from other countries in this story of persistence and courage in the face of horrible odds against survival.

—*Estelle Ford-Williamson*

Introduction

It was the end of the rainy season, the start of the dry. The long grasses our cattle grazed on were beginning to harden, and their green was draining away. Gunfire erupted; I could hear the sound of tanks and soldiers attacking our village some distance away, and smoke circled in the air. The war we'd been hearing about—a war on every southern Sudan village in a vicious attempt to control our people—had come to Adut Maguen, my home. With that fateful day, everything changed in my world, and a 14-year journey to find safety began.

I fled, and was joined by others: my great-uncle, a cousin, and two other boys, Matoc and Laat. We walked for months before finding a refugee camp, but that was not the end of our misery. Through the many changes and difficulties, my family's strong bonds and traditions kept me going, though there were many times it would have been easy to give up. The opportunity to come to the United States provided a safe home, but challenges followed as well. When the war finally ended and my friends and I made plans to return to find our families, I was prevented by not having travel documents arrive in time. I began writing this book so that I could deliver a message on paper I was not able to deliver personally to those in my country, especially the young.

This book details my life, but also the lives of other Lost Boys in order to update this story for the many who became interested when we first arrived in America. It shows the importance of tribal culture in helping us survive. It shows how we have become good Americans, but with a strong passion for those at home and a determination to build a new South Sudan through the knowledge and skills we are gaining here.

The book is also a call to correct the wrongs in Africa, to ensure that what happened to us does not happen to future generations. There are those who still suffer in active conflicts as well as in refugee camps, and we hope to help them.

South Sudan is a country with an economy based on cattle keeping and a society based largely in rural villages. Changes are coming. Oil is being developed, much-needed infrastructure is growing, but the growth will be guided by the culture's gifts: respect for what our elders tell us, working within the traditions of the cattle culture, consulting to avoid conflict, and believing we can develop our country and its rich resources while still treasuring and enhancing people's lives in the small villages.

We hope you will read with interest about a part of the world you may not know. And know that your support in buying this book will go toward improving lives in the small villages. Portions of the authors' earnings go toward building water wells and literacy programs in two area villages—mine and Stephen Chol Bayok's.

Thank you for reading our stories.

—Majok Marier

One

Don't Drink the Water

My first memory of the journey that was to last for many years was my uncle making a shoulder strap for a gourd and placing it on my chest. The whole thing scratched, as the strap was formed from twisted palm fronds, and they were very dry. They connected to a gourd that held my water supply. I didn't like the rig placed against my bare chest, and I tried to push it away.

While I struggled, my uncle looked at me through stern eyes, narrowed snake-like. Like most Dinka men who'd come of age, his lower teeth had been removed, a tribal custom. His mouth looked scary to me.

His brow carried six long scars, proud reminders of the ritual knife cuts and deep bleeding he withstood with no painkillers, marking his entry into manhood a few years before. There was no doubt my uncle was a strong warrior. But he must have sensed that he was going to use something other than force with his young nephew—actually his grand-nephew, as he was my grandmother's younger brother, part of a very large extended family I'd left behind.

I remember him telling me I would die if I did not have water. He was going to have to go on, and the others would also have to leave me, and I would die of thirst. He wasn't angry; he talked to me softly like he always did when he was trying to convince me of a logical way to do things.

I was little and my head barely reached the stomach of my grandmother's brother. Breathless from running down the path away from my village, I had come upon him in another group of people as I ran that morning. I had fled because the village was on fire—I could see huge

5

flames leap up over the tall grasses where my cattle grazed—and I knew that the war had come to Adut Maguen. I ran barefoot, frightened by fire and smoke and the sound of tanks and gunfire. War had been predicted, and that morning I heard the sound of it in my village. War was right there.

By noon I grew weary of the trek, and I was hobbling, trying to slow down. I encountered groups of men and women, other boys, people from other villages, but kept pushing on. When I saw the tall, lean figure of young Dut Machoul, I was glad to see an older person I knew.

I walked fast because I wanted to escape the Hummers and the smoke and tanks and gunfire, but my uncle, who was probably 17, with legs much longer than mine, quickly caught up. He then tried to help me with a supply of water.

I guess I did not want to carry something so scratchy, and I must have thought water would be ahead, and I'd get it when I needed it, but Dut set me straight right away. First he pulled me into the remains of a burned village to find dried gourds that had been part of someone's household. Then he made the makeshift rope to hold the gourd high up on my chest to allow my arms to swing with my steps.

After I'd finally agreed to wear the offending gourd, we stopped near a puddle of still, dirty water and he put water in the gourd.

I resisted again, because it was heavy across my chest. Again, he put me on the right path.

"You are not going to drink this water until you see the next water," he said. "You need to just wet your mouth with it. Until you see your next water, you must put only enough in your mouth to keep from getting too dry."

And that's what I did. If I'd not done that, running a water-soaked finger over the inside of my mouth on a regular basis, I may not have survived. Later the same day we encountered a cousin, Kau, and Dinka boys about my age, Matoc Kout and Laat Mathou. They were from the Rumbek area where I lived, but I did not know them before. Because they were Dinka, and we spoke the same dialect, we walked together. My uncle helped them with water gourds as well, and we journeyed long and hard together, eventually for a thousand miles through three countries.

During the many weeks and months of that dry season, without food, clean water, and without our families, we kept asking: When can we stop? When are we going to get to a place where we can rest? Where are we going? The answers might well have been "Never," and "There is

This is the way Majok's people build their homes in Pulkar, South Sudan—high up to escape lions and other predators.

no such place," and "We don't know." For we walked and walked for months and months, in the middle of the night, and late at night. We never knew the answer to the question: "How long can we stay?" For there were many reasons to pick up and run again.

I was seven years old in 1987, and my home was built up high to keep us safe from the lions that would roam the rural area outside Rumbek, Sudan, near where I was born. Our village, Adut Maguen, lay about eight miles southeast of Rumbek, and south of the village of Pacong. (All of this area lies in what is now officially the country of South Sudan, but the birth of that nation followed much suffering and death, and it is this story I will relate in the next pages.) In this small village, my mother took care of us, my older brother, my younger sister and younger brother and me. However, our fates changed when the war came to our village. The struggle that followed colored my entire life, as it tore apart my home village and thrust me onto a path I could never have imagined. I had to leave with other Lost Boys, to walk barefoot for years, exposed to lions, hyenas, enemy soldiers, hostile tribesmen, thirst and starvation. We spent most of our young lives in a search for food, water, and freedom.

While I have stopped walking across Africa and have settled here in the United States, I feel I am still on a journey, with a goal of making others see the conditions of the country I come from and the section of Africa I left. I also want to open others' eyes to the sometimes desperate situations once some help is found in refugee camps in an effort to improve the lot of those whose lives are deeply affected by those experiences.

And I want to detail what the Lost Boys are doing in America today and what our hopes are for our home country. We are men now, although we do not mind if you call us the Lost Boys. For this brings to memory the life-and-death struggle we faced as youths in Eastern Africa and reminds us that we have survived a brutal life, and have been very fortunate. We hope the way we live out our lives here in America reflects the gratitude we feel for this new life. Finally, I'd like to show how the bloody fire of the civil war flung us onto continents far away from our home, but we are forming a new generation of leaders for the new South Sudan that has been created out of our suffering.

Many people have heard of Darfur, which has been called a genocide; Darfur is located in the western part of Sudan. However, the tragic attacks in South Sudan predate the conflicts in Darfur, in my country's western section. I believe it is important that others know the details of the conflicts and become familiar with the causes and the impacts of these wars, as there is no hope for this large section of the African continent unless the world understands more.

Sudan, which spans both sides of the equator, was Africa's largest country until recently. In January of 2011, according to a peace agreement that concluded our bitter civil war and was signed in 2005, there was a vote to decide if Sudan should be two countries. The vote was overwhelmingly for independence, spelling a new day for the new nation of South Sudan. There is much to do to enhance the existing framework in our area to build our nation. Darfur remains another effect of the punishing Arabic regime in Khartoum, and it will be dealt with, as Darfurians are largely our African brothers and sisters. But first we need to set things right in South Sudan. The solution to one depends on the solution to the other.

I was one of tens of thousands of Sudanese boys who, when the conflicts between North and South that began in 1983 reached our village in 1987, began a long search for escape, a way to find food and water and to find peace that would enable us to survive, to grow into manhood. We eventually walked to Ethiopia where we found refugee camps. But we were forced back to Sudan because of Ethiopia's civil war, and sought shelter in Kenyan refugee camps for 10 years.

Most people became aware of the Lost Boys in 2001, when, like me, some of them began to arrive in the States. But their agony began in 1987 and did not end until 2001, when most were resettled here. Now we ache to solve the long-standing problems between peoples in our region that forced the journey in the first place. And we want to make sure that the deaths and suffering in refugee camps, a greater tragedy heaped on top of already tragic circumstances, don't continue in the future.

My life in my village, in the Lakes region eight miles east of Rumbek, consisted of tending cattle that my mother owned. My father died when I was very young, and I don't remember him. We lived in a village of about five hundred people, most joined in some way with others through marriages and blood relationships. Other family members around me were a grandmother and her brothers and their families, my mother's brothers and their families. We lived in two camps year round; we lived in our permanent home during the rainy season (thus the building above the ground—not only to avoid lions and other predators, but to escape the floods of water that would course through during heavy downpours). The rest of the year, usually from December to the end of March, we would create dry season camps near shrunken rivers so that we could have access to water for our animals and ourselves.

Our cattle are the focus of our lives. In Sudan, a person's wealth is completely tied to how many cattle he owns—rather, how many a *family* owns, as there's not a lot of distinction between the individual and the family. Cattle are acquired through marriage, and everyone marries. The haggling over cattle for a woman's bride-price, for instance, is a major community event, observed by all the village people. Everyone knows everyone's business in this village—and it is everyone's business, as many are related. But more about the bride-price and bride-wealth later.

On a typical day, at the age of seven, I would rise from a mat on the dirt floor where I'd slept matches-in-a-box style with my older and younger brother. My sister and mother would already be up, making a fire and beginning preparation for the meal that would be taken at lunch time by the rest of the family there in our home, and that would be carried by the rest of us to the grazing fields. There is no breakfast—we would go to the water source (pots of water that my mother and sister had

Young boys watching cattle near Pulkar, South Sudan, as Majok was doing in 1987 when the Sudanese Army attacked his village of Adut Maguen.

fetched), and wash our faces. My mother would have prepared our lunch to carry to the grazing fields with us.

My job was to untie the cattle and lead them to graze on the grasses not far from our home. I would do this with my older brother and my cousins. Twenty cattle had to be rounded up into groups, tethering them with ropes strung around their necks held like so many balloon strings. Once we were out on the grasslands, we'd make sure we had all our cattle in one location and keep an eye on them so that none strayed. We knew our cattle by color patterns. In fact, Dinka names are actually colors of cattle. My name, Majok, signifies a black and white pattern in Dinka.

When the cattle were settled in a particular area, we could relax some and play with other boys who were doing the same thing with their families' cattle. By about noon, we'd take out our first meal of the day, groundnut paste rolled in a banana leaf. Afterwards, we'd chew on a sorghum plant stem. These grazing fields were not rolling grasslands as you might picture in the American West or large pastures such as you see

Young Dinka in a cattle camp near Majok's village wears ashes for decoration and shows off his young bulls.

in rural Georgia and Tennessee or the Midwest states. Mostly they were areas of man-high grasses, which the cattle munched all day long.

I did not attend school, but schooling was planned for me because my older brother was not going to attend. In Dinka families, one son attends, usually the oldest. But for some reason, my brother was not going to school, and it was I, when I was of age, who was to travel to a school building about 12 miles from our village. Because of the dislocation caused by war, I first learned my ABCs in a refugee camp in Ethiopia, 300 miles from my home. And I learned English rather than Arabic as is the Sudanese custom.

That one day during the end of the rainy season, in October or November, my pastoral life changed. Tanks, Hummers, and soldiers of the Sudanese army began an assault on our village. They started from the police station, where soldiers from North Sudan were stationed. In the past, these stations often would be attacked by rebels, militiamen from the Southern Sudan tribes, the Sudanese Liberation Army. But there were no rebels around in our area when these attacks began—North Sudan was warring on South Sudan, and they used the excuse that rebels were hiding in our village to destroy it. In fact, at this time, the rebels were just across Sudan's borders with Kenya and Ethiopia, a distance of about 200 miles.

There was a great deal of noise, smoke, and confusion as tanks moved into the area outside the village. Bombs fell, soldiers burned huts, streams of choking, blinding smoke were everywhere and people were running, gathering everything they could: belongings, food, mats, on heads and underarms. Children cried. There was much scurrying about, screaming, mothers calling for children, children for their mothers.

But I was not in the village—I saw the smoke, heard the gunfire and shelling, and I just kept moving, looking for a safe place. I went to the next village and found only burned huts and scattered bowls used for cooking. There were old and young, men and women, girls and boys, people and cattle on the paths at first. I kept walking with no belongings, looking for a place. But everywhere there was smoke, fire, burned-out homes and the menace of soldiers. We'd go toward the trees, which at this time were losing their leaves, so they offered only a little cover. And there were dangerous animals where there were trees. We just kept walking, trying to avoid the green clothes of the military. We tried to find out what was happening, where we would be safe.

Pretty soon it was just young males as the women and girls could not keep up, and the men stayed behind with them trying to make a home wherever there were villages that were far away from our home and where locals would allow. The danger was everywhere—families could be wiped out as the soldiers advanced to these villages that hadn't been attacked. The villages could run out of food and send newcomers away.

Ethiopia was where most of the goods that came to our area came from; there was little trade from the North. The South has little connection to the North economically, culturally or socially, and the very bad roads in our area went east, not north. We knew not to go north, and certainly not to Rumbek, a large town, because that's where the attacks were spreading from. We decided to walk far, far away so that we would be away from danger, and then we would try to find food and shelter.

Grandmother's Words

My grandmother told me the civil war would come to our village. Even more important and powerful, she and my mother taught me many skills to survive on my own. In Dinka culture, children are trained how to be strong because their parents tell them that they do not know what can happen to them. Parents show their children many things that could happen in the future.

I recall my grandmother talking to me when there was an incident about a year before full-out war came to our area. Our small village, Adut Maguen, is south of a larger one, called Pacong. One night, at Pacong, rebels of the Sudanese People's Liberation Army (SPLA) attacked the police station. The government troops were occupying the station in a stepped-up effort to quell the rebels; the rebels, local tribesmen, were attacking the police station at night.

My grandmother heard gunshots, but I was sleeping. When I woke up my grandmother called me and asked me, "Did you hear a gun sound last night?"

"No, Momdit, I didn't. What happened?"

"Anyanya attacked Pacong last night," she said.

"What is Anyanya, Momdit?"

"They are people who fight the Arabs."

"Why did they attack the Arabs?"

"My grandson, you are young, you do not know Anyanya. If Anyanya is going to fight again, I will die before this war." (These were tribes that fought the Arabs in a civil war many years earlier than the civil war that caused me to leave my village. Anyanya was a combination of Nuer, Lotuko, Madi, and other groups as well as Dinka tribesmen that fought the Arabs from 1969 to 1972. During that war, the Sudanese Army (SA) descended on the village and killed indiscriminately.) She wanted to die rather than have the Army kill people as they did then.

My grandmother said that I would not die in this war, even though she would die. I remember my grandmother told me this war was going to kill many people, and some would leave the country. She took care of me well there in the village and showed me how I could live alone without a parent's support. She told me to stay happy no matter what bad situation I had.

She told me Dinka men were the strongest, smartest, tallest—handsome and proud.

"Do you know what Monyjang means?" A new word. It sounded like *mon yang*.

"No, Momdit."

"Monyjang is the only man of the men."

It was interesting for me to hear that name, and it made me proud to be Dinka. I believe cultures can help people to survive in difficult situations like what the Lost Boys and Lost Girls had in 15 years of journeying in South Sudan, Ethiopia, and Kenya. South Sudan has been rich in traditional activities, and this kept the boys and girls alive. I believe South Sudan's different tribes and traditional cultures keep the people together, and make their lives rich and exciting.

I do know that some people see us as funny because the Dinka men cannot cook, according to our culture. Women are the only ones who know how to cook in Dinka culture. This is a guideline of Dinka culture that keeps men away from the kitchen. We had many rules in our community to inspire people to work hard, learn responsibility and respect people. These rules led us to work hard in America. We are responsible people, and we help our own people, friends, relatives, family and parents.

Now, I do cook Dinka food for myself and for my fellow Lost Boys in Clarkston, Georgia. Our foods are usually rice with meat, chicken, and lots of vegetables. And I have a Dinka wife, and now a daughter, but I will not have two wives, as is the custom in my village. While I value much that is Dinka, I am changing a bit.

An outsider is probably confused by all the tribal names in the South Sudan area. It is probably not unlike the differences in regions here in the United States. I understand that there are great rivalries among football teams from different states or areas, such as Georgia vs. Florida, or Auburn vs. Alabama. Or you could think of very popular Super Bowl opponents. However, instead of playing games against each other, young men of the tribes in South Sudan were trained as warriors, and many have long traditions of fierce fighting to protect their various areas in South Sudan.

Something that is difficult to understand is the lengthy history of our culture. The Dinka and the tribes like them have been in existence since the time of the ancient Egyptians and before. There is a lot of focus on Egyptian culture, probably because of the exceptional pyramids, religious temples, and the pharaohs' burial sites that have yielded gold, pottery, mummies and many other persistent reminders of a long-ago culture. The excitement has been great, especially since the discovery of untold treasures in Tutankhamen's grave. But the sources of the Nile—the White Nile and Blue Nile, where many southern Sudan tribes live—were mostly unexplored by Europeans, the writers of much of the world's history, until only recently, relatively speaking.

—ᙡ—

HISTORY OF SUDAN AND EGYPT

Our knowledge of the history of the area of southern Sudan, including the Rumbek area that Majok comes from, is clouded by the absence of permanent structures and written records. Geography and tribal patterns of self-sufficiency kept the area isolated; yet cattle-keeping and other traditions are similar to those in Africa's oldest civilizations, and indications are that trading with other areas developed over the years. Yet until 1841, the White Nile area, a dense swamp inundated by floods from May to December every year, was never explored; only in that year did a Turkish viceroy of Egypt send an expedition through the White Nile and Blue Nile areas to find the headwaters of the river, in Uganda. European impacts followed.[1]

To understand southern Sudan, it's important to look at Sudan's history, and at Egypt's history as well. Since the early 1960s, studies of 20th century artifact rescues have yielded many new discoveries, and more are occurring every day.

It is well to remember that in ancient times, Egyptians and Nubians mingled in Egypt and in Nubia, and that Nubia's highly developed African culture rose before the ascent of the Egyptian dynasties. Some of the kings in ancient Egyptian times were from Nubia. The region was in what is now Sudan, north of present-day Khartoum, the country's capital. In the Old Testament, it was referred to as the Kingdom of Kush. Khartoum is at the juncture of the White Nile and Blue Nile rivers, which flow north and form the storied Nile River. Upper Nubia developed around the third and fourth cataracts of the Nile, and included the royal cities of Kerma and Meroe; Lower Nubia fell between the first and second cataracts; both areas offered access to much-prized gold fields and emerald mines, as well as a door to the valuable products of sub–Saharan Africa.

"Much material in Lower Nubia now lies under Lake Nasser, permanently flooded after the construction of the Aswan High Dam, while some Upper Nubian sites have been destroyed by the completion of the Merowe Dam at the Fourth Cataract," writes Marjorie M. Fisher, editor with others of Ancient Nubia: African Kingdoms on the Nile. *"Nubia's indigenous language, which might offer further insights, was not written down until the Meroitic Period (mid-third century BC to mid-fourth century AD), but the language, although deciphered, can be understood only to a very limited extent."*

So those wanting to understand about this culture "must explore the region's relations with Egypt, as well as the indigenous sources of data," Fisher writes.[2]

Researchers wanting to view the remains of the Nubian physical culture, fortunately, are able to see the remains documented and removed in several museum collections, including many in the United States. In the early 1960s, when the Aswan High Dam was being built, an effort to salvage artifacts was begun.

"Before the world lost much of its precious heritage, an international rescue campaign was organized under the auspices of the United Nations Scientific, Technical and Cultural Organization (UNESCO)," an article in American Visions *states. "Participating foreign missions were offered half of the discoveries that would otherwise have been permanently lost. Several American museums and universities participated in the UNESCO Salvage Campaign, and their share of finds forms the backbone of the major Nubian collections in this country.*

"The very concept of rescue archeology—and the foundations of the Nubian collections at the Boston Museum of Fine Arts, the University Museum of Archeology and Anthropology at the University of Pennsylvania, and the Oriental Museum of the University of Chicago—originated in Nubia at the beginning of the century, when the first (and smaller) dam was being erected near Aswan in 1906," the article continues, then details how these discoveries enabled the identification of several previously unknown cultures, and a completely new view of the Nubians, now seen to be rivals at times to Egyptian power.[3]

It is known that several of the ancient Egyptian gods such as Anubia, god of embalming,[4] *and Isis,*[5] *were Nubian. There were Nubians who were kings in Egypt, and Egyptian kings took Nubian wives. "Nubia appears not to have been exploited unduly by the Egyptians," who probably did not enslave Nubians, Fisher writes. "As late as the Old Kingdom, many Lower Nubian princes and princesses were raised in the Egyptian court.... The intention was that upon their return home, they would promote Egyptian culture in Nubia and alliances to Egypt."*[6] *Archaeologists of Egypt and Sub-Sahara Africa find a great many links between the cultures, starting from the time before the Sahara became the desert it is now, and before Arabic groups came to live between Egypt and Sudan. In a sense, Sudan is an important source of much that is Egyptian culture and geography.*

There was great interplay between Egypt in the north and Sudan as well as other areas of sub-Saharan Africa. In fact, all of what is now Africa shared much in customs, religion, and cultural objects. Archaeologists point to similarities between the early tools of the area, from bone harpoons to pottery bowls and jars, items that appeared from the Atlantic to the southern part of what is now the Sahara, on up along the Nile, finally reaching into Palestine, as well as similarities in the famous blue crown of Egyptian rulers of the New Kingdom era and the beaded miter crown used in Cameroon in the past (used ceremonially in present-day Nigeria). All of these examples simply suggest that there were ties between what may seem like unlike cultures, ties that date back to the Neolithic period.[7]

Yet to look at Sudan as a country today is to look at true contrast. Egypt was eventually ruled by Greek, Roman, Muslim, and Turkish regimes (The Ottoman Empire) before gaining independence. Largely through the dynasty begun with Khedive Muhammad Ali, the country was transformed on a European model.[8] Because of that influence, Egypt learned how to tame and dam the Upper Nile, and became (at least until the Arab spring of 2011) a secular country that is more developed than almost any other country on the African Continent; it sits at the north end of the Nile Valley, orienting itself to the Indo-European culture of the Mediterranean. Sudan to its south is a culturally, religiously, and ethnically split nation. Nubia was Christianized and remained that way from approximately AD 580 to 1400. At the end of this time, some areas still remained independent and Christian,[9] affecting southern Sudan even today. Arabs, who came in initially in the 7th century but did not exact control for several centuries,[10] occupy the north, including the Nubian Desert, the ancient kingdom of Kush, and the capital, Khartoum. The area to the south, inhabited by various African tribes including the Dinka, includes some fertile area, some desert, and what at one time was simply referred to as the Sudd, or Tremendous Swamp. In fact, the swamp is the largest in the world; in Arabic, its name translates as "obstacle," which it has been for those trying to access the vast lands along its edges.[11]

North Sudan is relatively developed and for years has received most of the infrastructure improvements in Sudan, and from colonial times to present has dominated the rest of the country; South Sudan consists of the areas west and east of the Sudd, and the Sudd itself.

This part was basically left unconquered when in the early 16th century Muslim armies controlled all lands bordering the Nile, Alexandria to Khartoum. The South was called Bilad al–Sudan, the "Land of the Blacks," and stayed unexplored until the 1840s when the Turkish Ottoman Empire, under Muhammad Ali, invaded and seized Africans as slaves.[12]

After Turkish captors, slave traders from North Sudan followed. The Dinka, major victims of slavery, call this the "time when the world was spoiled."[13] The slavery continued into the late 1800s even though the British, who had come into power in the area, tried to end the trafficking. In the 1880s, the British army was destroyed in a revolt by North Sudanese, but they held on into the 1900s, finally dividing the Muslim north from the south, whose dominant religions are traditional animist and Christian.[14] *The Christian tradition is a lingering effect of the Christianization of the three kingdoms of Nubia in about 580 AD. The era continued until 1400, when most of Nubia became Muslim.*[15] *(Their counterparts in southern Sudan retained their Christianity or their animist religion.) The British, in the 19th and 20th centuries, encouraged the autonomy of the south and encouraged Christian missionaries in the area. With the withdrawal of the British in the mid–20th century, several attempts were made for the South Sudanese to become independent.*[16]

Majok says that the Agar Dinka were not enslaved, and it is possible, given their remote location in the Sudd, and their ferocity as warriors, that they were able to elude capture. As Baker, the English explorer, wrote, "They are something superlative."[17] *With their very tall stature, and their tendency to color their hair orange, rub their bodies with ashes and indulge in intricate and showy body decoration, as well as their fearsome skill with spears and shields, they were probably a formidable foe. Not to mention the high jumping, part of the unique dance of this group of Dinka, but also very useful in battle. In addition, while the Europeans only in the 1840s discovered a way through the Sudd to the White Nile headwaters, doubtless the Dinka were skilled in plying those waters, and could use them to escape those pursuing them. The pages of* Warriors of the White Nile: The Dinka *provide a glimpse of very proud and complex traditions and ways of protecting themselves, much of which are present in other South Sudan tribes as well.*

There is no doubt that there are large divides between Sudan and South Sudan today, and it will be a struggle for either side for the South to achieve true independence. But that was the agreement that capped a series of protocols signed in Naivasha, Kenya, in 2005. The south and the north agreed after a twenty-year civil war to provide for an election to allow southerners to decide if they would like to be a separate country. On January 9, 2011, almost 99 percent of those voting approved the separation of South Sudan from Sudan, and the new country formally became independent on July 9, 2011.[18]

—⚏—

The vote for independence occurred in January 2011, and the country of South Sudan formed six months later, but already war has broken out over the oil fields that lie in South Sudan—the source of the North's wealth since the end of British ownership. Many challenges remain.

My country, South Sudan, as you might guess, is a tribal-based culture with few modern conveniences, and the life today, although there are many hundreds from my village who went missing or were killed in the 1983–2005 conflict, is not much different than it was before that. Any improvement would lessen the hard life and the illnesses that attack our people today. Wells for a supply of water would be nice, making unnecessary the hours-long trips to bring water back to the village for cleaning and cooking—the endless job of women. Then perhaps they would have time for schooling, a luxury for men and women, as even under the pre-independence system, only one son was able to attend the bush schools that offer rudimentary learning. A clinic would be helpful to treat the many illnesses coming from bad water: diarrhea and dysentery.

Former United States president Jimmy Carter has a personal goal of eradicating the guinea worm, a painful highly replicating worm that lives in the pools of water that are cooking and bathing sources in our environment. He hopes the election aftermath and the new independence for South Sudan will not mean an interruption to his goal of outliving the last guinea worm. Malaria is on the rise in Sudan; underground pumps are needed to replace the stagnant water that attracts mosquitoes, for even though there have been tremendous efforts to supply our people with bedding nets to keep out mosquitoes, the water sits in pools, when it is available in the rainy season, and attracts these disease-bearing insects. Such wells will be very expensive to drill, as the water lies far, far below the surface.

Telecommunications in the form of cell phones and Internet would be good. There are a few satellite phones now where there were not before, and it is helpful to be able to contact neighbors and family, especially in an emergency, for going to the hospital. But first the basics: water, health, and a stable country.

If there were water to carry my people through the dry season—January, February, and March—then they would not need to move their homes every year, to go to an area closer to the rivers for water. It is a major undertaking to leave the elevated homes in my village and then travel to the new location. There the people must go gather the grasses and create the mud to make the new huts, create the new kitchens and gardens, and then move back to our home village three months later. These improvements would mean changes to the Dinka culture, for it is a culture accustomed to moving every year, but it would be made up for in greater education and innovation in ways of doing things.

I think the Dinka, the man among the men, will be adept at creating new ways of living, but will still retain his strong values of helping family, respect for others, and especially, depending on our elders for guidance as we go through these changes. Just as my grandmother prepared me for the war that tore away my home, wisdom such as hers will prepare us for the future.

In every culture there is probably a tradition of observing that life has many sorrows, but that it has joys as well. The Book of Ecclesiastes relates that there is a time for having plenty, and a time for losing all one has; "a time for weeping and a time for laughing; a time to mourn and a time to dance." My story here will be filled with instances that show the desperate situation we were in, yet there was sometimes a small blessing amongst the pain. One of those blessings was my great-uncle, a young man himself of 17 or 20, who accompanied us on the first journey, to Ethiopia, and showed us ways to stay safe. Our cousin, Kau, was a grace. Another was the care my family took to educate me, a small Dinka boy, on ways to do for myself. Many times I recalled my mother's and grand-mother's words as I looked for water, searched for food, tried to keep hope. They had made sure I would be ready for whatever happened to me. They could never have foreseen this story of incredible suffering.

Another blessing is that, early on, my uncle, Kau Raik, and I encoun-tered good Dinka companions, Matoc and Laat, and we all stayed together through the long journey to Ethiopia. We spoke mostly the same dialect, but we had some words that were different, so we came up with our own words or agreed upon a word when we had different names for the same thing. Language was a matter of life and death. If you traveled with people who spoke a different language, they could plot against you, even kill you.

There was enough death around, and we often came near death our-selves. Sometimes we would see a person lying beside the path. We were not sure if he or she was alive or dead.

"He is only sleeping," Matoc, who was older than I, said. In fact, people did lie down to rest. Sometimes they pulled off from a group and said they were going to rest. But often they never got up.

My uncle, Kau, Matoc, and I, and Laat, who at six years old was even younger than I, always made sure we pulled each other up to continue walking. If we had not done this, any of us could have died.

In order to hide from the tanks and Hummers and SA soldiers, and also to keep from running into people who might do us harm, we walked off the main road where tanks were forced to travel, and we walked at night and early morning. This also kept us out of the hottest part of the day, which would be deadly to us. We never had enough water or food. We walked until midnight the night before, and then slept for a couple of hours, rose and ate some kind of food, maybe sorghum grains or corn we'd been able to find, then left at four in the morning to walk for six more hours. During the middle of the day, we rested under a tree well off the path where others might find us.

Often I found we were under a tree that was like a tree from my own village. Other times I noticed that there were mountains in the distance, which I had not seen from my own village. The land always had interesting things to see. I'd rise before dawn as usual with the others, have some boiled grain over fire, and clean my teeth with ashes from the fire (we Dinka use ashes for toothpaste and many other purposes, often to decorate our skin for ceremonies). Once or twice I remember I'd be sleepily making my way down the path. All of us would be quiet, still a little asleep, and the sunrise would start filling the land to the east with light. That was a good feeling, because it told us we were going in the right direction—Ethiopia was east, where the sun rose. And there was such light over tall fields of drying grasses that my breath hardly came. With the heat of the day yet to come, I could enjoy the beauty of my country. It would be enough to help me move my legs and walk fast, to feel that slightly cool air and see the slanted golden light of sunrise over the fields and paths I would need to walk for the next several hours.

But most of the time, there was no time to think of beauty. There was only desperation.

Two

Walking in the Wild

A man and his wife were out in the bush walking to a village near their home, passing through thickets of trees and high grass. They had their baby with them, the wife carrying it in a sturdy calfskin sling across her body. All of a sudden, an elephant appeared in the forest, all by itself. It charged toward the man and woman, and grabbed the man and wrapped him with his trunk, raised him high in the air, and then threw him to the ground, killing him. The woman ran, but the elephant caught up with her and tossed her in the air. As it did so, the baby and heavy sling flew off her body and the skin was caught on the limb of a tree. Villagers came by and found the baby, and it lived, though both parents died.

This incident took place in my village before the war, and I grew up hearing it as a caution for watching out for solitary animals. It was a story I related to my companions often during our long journey. Animals in groups are usually not a problem, because they are following a dominant leader, or staying together for protection. A herd or a group of elephants doesn't present a danger because they are following the leader, but an animal alone is another matter. A solitary animal most often has been forced out of the herd because it's violent and a danger to the others, and it's a great risk to humans.

Wild animals, including lions and hyenas and elephants, as well as snakes and scorpions, were our greatest predators on our journey, as were hunger and thirst. Sometimes other people were predators as well, but I will tell more later about the human threats. It took a great deal of knowledge to assess how to deal with each of these. As we walked, we shared

Majok on 2010 trip near Pulkar on a path similar to those they took while fleeing burning villages in 1987.

stories like this and discussed who and what to look out for. That was the way we survived.

Villages throughout southern Sudan were burning, and everyone was fleeing, when I started out with my uncle and later found Kau. People were frantic, trying to get away from the war, just as we were. Some carried bundles, mothers towed children by hand and on the breast, fathers herded an occasional cow until they finally had to leave it by the side of the path. Most carried gourds full of grain and water for sustenance. Most were Dinka, but did not speak our dialect. If people we encountered did not speak our language, we hesitated to become friends with them, because they could trick us by speaking strange words to each other. We wouldn't know if they were plotting to harm us, or talking about finding water. We would hurry ahead. But still we would stop where a group of people was gathered on the ground when we needed to rest. Others would be resting, too, each home group arranged around its own tree, and we would be under a separate tree.

In one of these stops we heard boys like me speaking our dialect. We talked, and I found out one spoke our Agar subtribe dialect, so he was of our people. Another boy in the group of people sitting in that group picked up on our conversation and he also spoke the same way. The first boy was Matoc, and the second was Laat. They were from an area near Rumbek, but not our village. When we talked more, we found that we did the same thing back home—watched cattle. And that we enjoyed playing the same games with other boys while we grazed cattle.

For instance, we all knew a kind of tree that produced gum, and we would collect the goo, roll it up and form a ball, and hit it with a stick to move it forward. In the game, called *adeir*, we would push the ball with a stick with teams of 10 on each side, pushing the ball to a goal. Or we would make shields out of plum-tree wood and practice war with sticks and shields, an imitation of the buffalo-skin shield our Dinka warriors used.

We decided we would walk together, and I was glad to have companions my age. My uncle told the other boys to go gather some palm leaves by the path, and my uncle braided palm rope he later attached to squash gourds for Matoc and Laat to carry water. The walking was much easier with my friends.

The talk as we made our way east on the path was about the dangers around us. The Sudanese Army had attacked our villages, and we didn't know if we might meet them again. The Army could only move on the main road (there are only a few roads that tanks can move on in South Sudan), and so we walked on paths that avoided the road. People we encountered would tell us, if we could understand their dialect, where there were soldiers, or where there were animals about.

"Watch out for the green clothes," we'd tell each other, as the SA wore light green fatigues. We'd try to stay near trees, even though now in the dry season the leaves were dried and thin. At least they provided some cover.

Next to those humans, our greatest fear was lions. Back in our villages, all of our homes were built up over the ground and we accessed them by ladders, primarily because of the floods that came in the rainy season, but also because of the lions. We kept dogs to ward off the hyenas and the lions. The lions usually were active around five o'clock in the evening, so we looked out for them. But if we saw hyenas, we were safe, for they kept the lions at bay.

At that time, we thought hyenas would not kill a man, only other animals, but later, in 1989, while we were in Pinyudo camp in Ethiopia, a man was killed near my home in southern Sudan by a hyena, but I did not know this until people told me this in my village after the war. So now we know to fear them, too. But as we set out on our journey away from the SA soldiers' attacks, we thought a hyena would be protection against the fearsome cats, for they prey on them. Besides lions, hyenas go after cattle, goats, and our own dogs.

For such a small animal compared with a lion, a hyena, with its sloping back and oversized head, has tremendous power. A hyena can attack and kill a larger animal by the sheer force of its jaws. Once a hyena locks those teeth into a prey, the wounded animal jerks and runs and turns about trying to get free. The hyena just hangs on with those clenching jaws, letting the intense struggle work to his advantage; the animal will weaken and eventually die as the hyena rips the prey's skin and limbs in the fight. So lions will flee hyenas, hyenas will be discouraged by dogs, and lions will avoid either of the other two. But we never knew what could happen in the bush. We had little protection, other than the trees with their drying leaves.

This lesson from the animals helped us later in Pinyudo, as some monkeys screeched loudly high in trees above us when we were left on our own to search for grasses to make our shelters. They made such a racket that we knew to be afraid and look for a lion or other danger. The monkeys were alarmed by wild animals in the area, and they were signaling each other. And we were afraid because we were lost. But I'll relate more about this experience, as it shows that even when we were in refugee camps, we were not safe from wild animals.

That night, my uncle also showed us how we would travel to keep alive. If we walked during the heat of the day, we could die from thirst and exhaustion, and also were more likely to be seen by the Sudanese Army, so we found a place where we could crush long grasses and sleep. We did not eat; I had eaten a paste of ground nuts in a banana leaf earlier in the day, and that was my food. That night and every night afterward, we rose about 4 a.m. and walked while it was cool and dark. We walked for eight hours, and then we rested in the middle of the day, usually under a tree, one that was far off the path so we would not be found by others. We would find some grain, sorghum wheat, or corn, among the harvested stalks in plots on the edges of settlements we passed, although these villages were mostly burned; we parched the sorghum seeds and boiled them with the corn for lunch, then rested more and then walked in the late afternoon until about midnight. Then we slept again and woke at four or so to be on our way.

A stranger might join us while we were walking, but we were careful who we allowed to join us. We would always ask, "Why are you here?" "Where are you from?" "What tribe are you?" If his story sounded like ours, that he was fleeing the soldiers, and he seemed to know the names of local villages, then we would allow him to walk with us. Sometimes we did not have a good feeling about a person, as though he could be a soldier or another enemy. When we stopped to rest, my uncle or I would suddenly jump up and say, "Let's go!" and then we five would walk quickly away, as though we had to go fast. Usually that worked to keep us safe.

The next morning after our first day on the path, we rose and walked in darkness. We did not know the country, we did not know the threats, but we kept walking so that we could get as far away from the shelling and killing as we could. We had talked to people on the path the day before and we heard there were refugee camps in Ethiopia. That was many, many days away, and we knew it would be an extremely long trip, even if we had no obstacles. On a straight line, it is probably a distance of 400 miles, although we had no way of knowing it at the time. And there were plenty of problems.

On the third day, we came to a village, Pankar, and the houses there, like many in that area, were built up high. We arrived at night, so we did not see the land around. We were among a group of people who had been traveling together, even though we did not talk with those whose language we did not share. The villagers allowed us to sleep under their homes, where the children slept. The rest of the group slept out from the houses in nearby fields. In the middle of the night, we all woke up when a lioness stole under the house and tried to grab one of the children. We screamed, and the lion roared, then ran away. Everyone was suddenly up, and frightened for their lives. All were running around screaming, trying to see where the animal was. There were SPLA soldiers in the area who came to help when they heard the lion and the sound of people crying; they went looking for the lion and its mate. Often the male lion is in the grasses waiting while a female attacks, and the male catches those running away. But the soldiers found no lions.

At the suggestion of the villagers, all the children and we three boys and my uncle and those who were sleeping under their houses moved inside, and all those sleeping in the fields moved into the space under the houses. The lion did not roar again, but it was a scary night.

Sometimes in those first days we walked in a group of as many as fifty to a hundred people. There was not much talking back and forth as we did not understand their language, but they were mostly Dinka. Whenever we would stop to rest, the groups sat under trees based on their home. They were there; we were here; we did not mingle. I understand weddings and family gatherings in America can be like this; one may wonder about who those other people are, but people in the bride's family gather in one area, and same for the groom's, and within these groups sometimes there are other subgroups that mostly talk to each other.

The Dinka is a very large tribe in Sudan, and it is only in Sudan. It is not in other countries. But there are many subgroups of Dinka, such as my group, the Agar Dinka, and within the Agar Dinka there are Agar Dinka and other Agar Dinka; I was from a village north of Pacong, and Laat was from another village south of Pacong. Matoc and my uncle were from a settlement south of Pacong, but we are all Agar Dinka. There are also subtribes of Dinka such as the Cic, and Aliab; I could not understand the language of any of these. There are other subtribes: Rek, Malual, Tuic, and Gok. At the time I could not understand these, but as a result of my experiences over the years with different dialects, I am able to understand these Dinka languages.

It's as though the experience of the Civil War and displacement in refugee camps created a common language, as if at the wedding mentioned above, all the guests were told they must dance with each other and in the process they found they had many things in common and became fast friends afterwards.

Southern Sudan has been known as the Sudd, or swamp, through history. It's the land at the upper end of the White Nile River, surrounded by swampy areas that often slow this giant river's flow. Every schoolchild learns the Nile is the world's longest river, and it is generally considered the longest at 4,130 miles, or 6,650 kilometers. From southern Sudan to a point north where the Sobat River joins it, the White Nile is surrounded by reed-choked backwaters. During the dry season, one can walk through this area, but during the rainy season one cannot. This was beginning of the dry season, so we could walk a good part of the way through the river country.

Before reaching the Nile we had to cross two other rivers. When we reached the Na'am River, which is not too far from Pacong, we swam across it. As young children, we learned to swim in the Na'am, and that helped

This is Majok standing beside the River Na'am, near the site of Adut Maguen village, with a relative. This was the first river they had to cross while escaping the village firing.

us in our journey as we did not have to search for a way across. Similarly, we crossed the Payii River. I understand many American children do not learn to swim, and this is a great disadvantage to them, I think, because in this life-and-death emergency, we were able to cross on our own.

We passed through areas where the people were Dinka, but of a different subtribe. We were Agar Dinka; these were Cic. We stayed in a Cic village named Tod. Then we moved to an Aliab area—those people actually spoke our dialect—and spent three days in one of the villages called Panliet.

Since I had left my village, Adut Maguen, this next part of the journey was the hardest. The Nile is very broad, especially as there are swamp areas adjacent. There are mosquitoes on the Nile that will eat people alive, but we had no mosquito nets, blankets, bedsheets, or houses to protect us. It was not possible to swim; we had to wait for a local boat, and that took three days of waiting. In that time, we had no food to eat that would help resist the effects of the mosquito attacks. Many people got sick immediately because of the insect assaults. It was now a week since I had left my home, and it was starting to be very difficult; I had never experienced anything like this in my young life.

The Nile, which has miles-wide swamps and very swift tributaries, presented a real challenge. The streams going into the Nile are very fast. Three or four miles upstream from the Nile, these tributaries are easy to cross. But near the Nile, the stream might be as wide as a large dining room table is long, but very swift. A man who was part of the larger group we were with jumped in to swim across and he emerged completely naked. The rest of the group laughed at him, saying "Don't try that again!"

So we had to wait for a boat that could take us across. And we had to cross the Nile in stages, because of the streams. It took us a total of three days. We started out at 2 p.m. at a place called Achum Shore. We crossed that swamp and eventually came to the actual River Nile. It took all day to cross, and we spent the night on the other side. We had to cross water again because there was a branch coming out of the Nile that had a very high current. We found another stream and crossed that as well. After that, we found a way to get out. It was actually a large swamp.

There was mud and a lot of tall grass. We didn't get a boat, so we walked through that mud all day and came out in the evening. We wore a brown gooey mess on our bodies. This kind of stream was different from that formed on the inside of the river where currents could be very fast. The swampy expanses just flowed out of the river and just died somewhere. The water stayed there, stagnant. Everywhere you go in that area, there is a lot of water.

Once on the other side, we walked again, still avoiding the main road that the SA tanks and Hummers could travel. We crossed the road at night, and continued on walking for several days until we reached Poktub, where there was construction activity, now halted, for the building of the Jonglei Canal, a huge project involving Egypt and Sudan. This canal was to be 224 miles long, would connect two sections of the White Nile, and enable some water that now goes to Egypt, which, by law, gets most of the water, to be diverted and channeled into many communities in South Sudan. While it seems to be for a good cause, there are many problems with the project, chiefly that the South Sudanese have never been allowed to be at the table during any of the planning. They want to discuss possible impacts on their entire section of Sudan and its alteration of patterns of life throughout the area. The project stopped in 1983 when the war broke out and has not been resumed.

Majok amid sorghum grain growing near Pulkar, South Sudan. Plants were sustenance on much of the journey.

But there was activity in Poktub; we could get food. All along our journey so far we had been limited to boiling corn and the parched seeds from sorghum stalks near our route. One time a day only, when we stopped around noon, we ate these meager rations. Poktub was the site of extensive roads, cranes and bulldozers, all assembled for the project, even though now they were mostly still. There were people who would give us food, or allow us to trade work for food, and so we stayed there three days, gathering our energy and filling our bellies. We were able to get squashes and groundnuts and other foods we had not eaten since we were in our villages.

Our goal was to get to Ethiopia, because we kept hearing there was a refugee camp there. The Arabs could not reach us in Ethiopia, and we could grow to manhood and go to school. Yet there was a large desert between us and the border. It was important to replenish our energies before making that trip. We needed to find some way of staying more than a night or two. For the first time, we were able to devise a way to stay in a location long enough to get plenty of food and water and rest.

For the first time, because we were good inventors, we created a kind of home for three months.

What we found was that there was a lot of metal trash there due to the construction project—building materials, old tires. We learned we could take a sheet of discarded iron, beat it into a bowl shape and then make handles from other iron scraps. Residents could pour durra wheat and sorghum into the pan. They would give us grain in this pot—and then we would give them the pot. They didn't have a way to go to town and get things they could cook with. They had to cook with clay pots, and these had to be replaced often due to burning. And we needed the grain to eat.

That is the way we survived that area. We tried, but there was nothing we could do, workwise. If you went to local people and said you needed food, today they would give you something, but tomorrow they would say, no, we don't know you. So we came up with this way to create a chisel and then we used it to cut the other tools, and then we made the pots.

The local people in Poktub called these pots "Bahr el Ghazal." Dinka people live together in their own communities, and they want to know where you are from. If you go to the north, they know you are from the south, and they want to know your region. So they named us the Bahr El Ghazal because that is our region in Sudan. And they gave the same name to the pots.

We also made sandals from the rubber tires. I understand Americans call these "Jesus boots." They are a flat sole with loops attached for the big toe (what we call the "big thumb") and a strip across the middle of the foot. These pieces we nailed to the sole. The shoes were very practical and they would not come off the foot. We had two different styles.

The residents loved our products, and the community benefitted. We even developed a pan large enough to cook a goat. With these products, we could trade for grain and other foods to eat.

Our housing there was an abandoned steel cargo container. It became very hot during the day because the weather near Ethiopia was very hot. We couldn't go in the container, it was so hot. At night it would get really cold; but we had no choice. At least we were safe, and we managed to stay in one place while we prepared our bodies for the difficult desert crossing.

But always there was the question of where we would go if things became less friendly there. We knew they'd soon have all the pots and sandals they needed, so we made plans to leave.

We were all set to leave to walk to the next place, and all of this was in preparation for reaching the very difficult desert areas nearer the Ethiopian border. Just as we were preparing to leave, the construction site caught fire, and the residents told us we had to put out the fire. There were no buckets, or anything with which to put out the fire. We had to carry water from the river to the fire in just our hands, and that did not do much good. Still, when we tried to leave, the people told us we could not leave or they would beat us or worse, so we had to keep at it. We ran back and forth, back and forth, from river to fire, and only after three hours were we able to put it out. We were very late starting on our journey for that day.

It was from this time that we entered Nuer territory; those are lands held by the Nuer, a separate tribe from the Dinka, and there is a history of enmity between the two. Over time, territories for each group have been worked out, but when one group comes among the other tribe, there is often trouble. Each village we came to was burned out. We walked in that area for seven days, and everywhere the villages were burned. On this first part of our trip into the Nuer area, we were so late that we had to walk from midnight to 4 a.m. We rested until dawn, and then rose and tried to get water, but they would not allow us to get water; some boys with spears were ranged around the water well.

Instead, they forced us to walk further away—a distance of four hours—to get water. This was in an opposite direction for our path eastward, so we basically had to rest, go walk eight hours to get water and come back, and then go through the whole process again. We did this for several days, trying to get enough water in our bodies to withstand the heat of the desert that was up ahead. So we circled around for several weeks, never making headway to our destination. But the people would not allow us to use their water.

In Sudan, most of the villages have been settled and claimed by custom, but most have been uprooted and moved due to dire weather conditions, war, or other reasons. There are not firm government borders as there are in U.S. cities and towns. An area is defined by a tribe or clan establishing itself—often running off another, weaker group. So when a small group of strangers such as us arrived in their midst, the reaction of local villagers was suspicion. If five came now, then how many of our people were following, just waiting to take over the area? So staying very long in one place was not possible. The more we needed of their precious resources, the more worried they were and the more aggressive they became in seeing us gone. This pattern repeated itself in many communities, because in Sudan as in much of Africa there is such competition for water, food, land, and other resources.

The next part of my story shows this in horrid detail. When we were finally able to start on our journey to the desert, we experienced the most difficult conditions: we had to walk for two weeks, and for three days we saw no water at all. I had followed the advice of my uncle, Dut Machoul, to not drink water until we could see water, but to only wet the inside of my mouth, with the water I had. However, we wondered what would happen in the desert, as it was even dryer than the place where we were. And there were violent people who lived in the desert, or who may be traveling through.

We walked for two days in the Akobo Desert; we were without any water for eight hours, and we were very, very thirsty and weak because of the intense heat and thirst. Then a scene unfolded that could never have been imagined. We came upon a pool in the middle of the desert at Dochan, but we found there had just been a battle between enemy tribes fighting for the water, and there were dead bodies all over the land near the water.

Later, I found out that the Nuer people heard we were coming and that they came to the pool because of us. They heard we were walking and coming to this area so they were waiting for us because they thought we might have a lot of valuable things they could take from us. But they found instead the Murle people, their enemies they often fight—raiding each other's cattle—so they fought there at the pool and then they ran away, leaving the bodies of the dead.

We were just going to sit under a tree around the pool that was clean, with no dead people near it. It was really troubling for me to see a dead person for the first time in my life. Dut Machoul told me that if I did not make myself strong and ignore the bodies, then I would die like those people lying there. That made me think of how I could improve myself to be active all the time, to be the most active person in our group. We stayed there for several hours, but left as soon as possible. The place smelled bad and we feared for an attack that could occur some time sooner or later.

A man who was also resting beside the pool told us which way to go after we left the pool so we could avoid hostile locals. Not only that, he had a gun with him, and he killed antelope that had come to drink from the river. So on that day, we cooked and ate meat that he gave us. Fortified with water and meat, we embarked on what we hoped would be the last leg of the trip inside Sudan.

This part of the trip was one of the most difficult. We ran low on water and food, but we were pushing hard to gain the Ethiopian border. After a day and a half past the pool at Dochan we totally ran out of water, so we drank our own urine. We were very close to another of the main threats to our lives on the journey. In addition to wild animals, thirst, enemy soldiers, starvation, and unfriendly natives, there was one other killer: loss of hope. We were close to it.

We could not wait to leave Sudan. The government had declared sharia law in 1983, and years later it had reached our village and the rest of southern Sudan. Basically, that meant we had to accept Muslim law, and only believers in that faith have rights in that government. The attacks were meant to drive out all who did not accept the Islamic faith. All through this section of our country we saw only burned villages, and we'd walked with hundreds of people fleeing the scorched lands. It could only be better in Ethiopia.

When I think of the joys and sorrows aspect of our story, I can think of many sorrows, especially seeing my first dead person killed in fighting. But there were blessings, too: my uncle and his care, the fact that we'd narrowly missed what could have been a massacre of all of us if we'd arrived just an hour earlier at the pool. Instead of allowing me to be disheartened by what I saw, my uncle encouraged me to make myself strong and forget the bodies, and I learned to take action to overcome the problems of my surroundings, lessons that continue to help me. Despite the extreme hardships, I was learning a great deal, and becoming a strong Dinka.

"He is only sleeping."

That's what Matoc said as we passed a prone body there in the desert. He was saying what we told each other now when we saw a person lying by the side of the path. We were not sure if they were dead or alive. In fact, people did lie down to rest. Sometimes they peeled off from a group and said they were going to rest. But they never got up.

"Maybe he will feel better," Dut Machoul said once when a sleeping figure appeared on the right side of the path.

He stopped in front of me and put his hand on my shoulder, my skin sweating even at this early hour in the desert.

"Never give in to bad thoughts, never give up hope," he said. "You will die."

My uncle, like most people among the Dinka, had no teeth on the lower level of his mouth. In my culture, the lower teeth are thought to be sources of infection, and so these are extracted when a boy or girl is about 10–12 years old. He looked at me in such a serious way. But I heard his lesson.

"Yes, Uncle," I replied.

"You must harden yourself against the sad feelings that come when you see someone like that," he said, motioning with long arms to the right side of the road.

I kept walking. Moving seemed to help with the feelings.

"If you cannot harden your feelings, you will die like him," Dut Machoul said. I could sense my companions by my side at this point. I needed them to hear the message as well.

"Yes, Uncle."

I did not want to die.

The threats we faced were wild animals, thirst, starvation, unfriendly natives, and loss of hope. These were the problems we faced on the walk; but there were human challenges later from places we did not expect: the refugee camp organizers. Later, I'll tell how the humanitarian aid agencies often made things more complicated in our already difficult lives. Fortunately, despite being thrown into one bad situation, because we knew how to recognize dangerous animals, we were able to save ourselves.

While we were on the long journey to Ethiopia, the one that ended in this United Nations High Commissioner for Refugees (UNHCR) camp, there were more challenges. In the desert, we had very little food, only the remains of small amounts of boiled corn and grain. There were times we wanted to lie down and not get up, and we took turns pushing each other to our feet to keep going.

My two friends and my uncle, Kau, and I learned to adapt to the dangers and hardships of our trip by distracting ourselves with games, usually guessing games, and with singing songs we remembered from our villages. Those were the joys among the sorrows of our situation. We could play "guess what the camp will look like," "guess who we will see there," "guess what we will eat"—we spent a lot of time talking about food. We guessed what we would do there. We guessed when we would see our families next. We tried to imagine what our families were doing without us. When those games got started, we quickly changed so we wouldn't miss our families so much. We'd begin singing songs that we used to sing while watching the cattle. There were traditional songs about the cattle, and the village. The longest songs were those we made up as if we were courting a young lady in the village. It is traditional when wanting to marry a girl that a young man will make up songs to sing her that honor her, describe her beauty, and promise all sorts of things to her so she will select him as a husband. There is a great deal of teasing and making up songs that goes into the courtship process, so creating these songs took a lot of our walking time.

Mostly we learned to not think about the dead bodies we saw, and not to make ourselves unhappy thinking about family and the sustenance we lacked. Mostly we just kept walking and talking and singing.

Three

Where Was the World While We Walked?

We struggled to gain the distance between the Akobo Desert and our next goal—the border between Sudan and Ethiopia. We knew we would be safer there, at least from attacks by the soldiers. We would still have to find the refugee camp, and we would still have to worry about food and carrying enough water until we got there. We had not had any food for the last few days, and we had no water.

The only lands I'd ever known were flat and almost unvarying in height or features. In my home area, there were some changes that occurred in the dry season—the few water sources dried up, and a river bed became a wide, long gully. Nevertheless, I'd never seen other geographic features like desert or mountains. This long journey changed all that. The desert had brought us hot sands and land that was not only flat, but had no trees at all. Trees were a food source for us on the first part of the journey, because we could exist on the pulp of the shea butter fruit, and we'd taken millet grain where we'd found it growing. We survived in the desert on grains of sorghum we'd stored in our gourds. Here there was nothing else to eat, nothing to drink. But we kept up our songs and our stories to keep hope going, as there was very little else between us and illness and death.

For the first time, we followed a road, one that would take us from the desert toward Akobo, the final Sudanese settlement before Ethiopia. We joined this road between Nasir and Akobo when we crossed it south of Nasir. I'm not sure why we felt safe enough to travel a road, a rarity in this part of Africa. Perhaps we felt the soldiers would not be there, as it was not near a town.

Our songs and stories were our means of taking our minds off our miseries. Also, while we walked, we asked questions of each other. Where was the rest of the world while we walked? Did the world know what was going on? Surely there had been news stories about the awful bombings and all these Sudanese in search of safety. While we didn't have electricity and TV, our villages' transistor radios would bring us news of other countries. We knew of the United States and Great Britain and South Africa and many other countries with many resources. Why weren't they sending planes to bomb the Sudanese capital, where the enemy was coming from? Why weren't they bringing food and medicine to us, trying to find us? They had many more ways of finding us than we did of locating the aid.

Along the way, my uncle would sometimes talk with some of the seven who were traveling the same road nearby. Now, we made a shift. Rather than going to the town of Akobo, we would make a left turn and go toward the Akobo River. We were going to avoid the town because there were soldiers. My uncle said he'd heard we were now about four or five hours from the town.

Suddenly, after we've turned left toward Ethiopia and walked for several hours, a bountiful water source, the Akobo River, was in front of us. At the river, we swam across, determined to reach Ethiopia. At least now we have water.

The river was easy to cross here; there was no current, and we reached the other side with little difficulty. I wondered at why this river is so calm when it took us so long to cross the White Nile and all its tributaries and swamps. But we were grateful to be across—wet, exhausted, but happy. I mentioned before how Dinka children are all able to swim, a major help in our lives in the bush. We could have died had we not been able to swim across that day, because of the long journey and months of lack of water, food, and decent rest. We thought we could find food and water and safety if we could just get to Ethiopia and walk to the refugee camps. The hope of this is what kept us alive.

As we walked toward the town that was on the other side—Turgol, Ethiopia—I discovered that when I went to the side to pee, I peed blood. This frightened me. I told my uncle, and he said I would get better. I had bled from my feet lots of times, as most of us had. But this was a new worry.

At Turgol, we were able to get food—the villagers gave us maize, what Western people call corn. We boiled the grains, and then we took them with us on our journey. We had no salt, no oil, nothing. We just boiled our maize and went. The people that were here were Nuer, so they were not our tribe. We knew not to stay there. In Ethiopia, we were safe from the soldiers and tanks and guns, but we were not among people we knew there. So we kept walking.

We rose at 4 a.m. as we usually did when traveling, but we followed along the river for a long while. Our goal was a refugee camp we'd heard about, at Itang, in the north of a section of western Ethiopia that forms a thumb as it juts into Sudan. The thumb is created by a large curve in the Akobo River, and we were following that river, but now were in Ethiopia. We felt safer, because Ethiopia was friendly toward the SPLA and the southern Sudanese.

We were so glad to have water, to be in the sight of water after all the days struggling through the desert. My pee returned to normal. We could drink all the water we wanted, and store enough in our gourds for the road ahead. After about two hours, as dawn approached, we turned east toward Itang.

As we walked, I noticed that in this part of Ethiopia there were few trees. There was a thorn tree that does not produce anything. The only tree that they have here besides that is a palm tree. We have that tree in my village, but it is not the only thing we have. We have another called the thou tree, and you get it in dry season. We have another fruit called chum that grows in the dry season. We have a plum tree. During May, it would get fruit. It is different from plums you have in the United States. It will make three seeds, and then you beat it so you have juice and you put it in water and you can drink it. This is a good tree.

But in the area we were passing through, it was dry season, and even the palms were not so green. And there were few of them. When we eventually found villages—the villages were about a day apart—there were no tall trees. We just saw houses, and bushes, but there were no trees like back in my village. Also, there were few of the tall grasses like the ones we have. The areas we were walking through, they didn't have that kind of thing.

Trees were important in our journey for safety. If a stranger came toward us, we could hide. Most important, we could rest during the afternoon, the hot part of the day, without someone traveling on the road seeing us, and us having the advantage of shade to cool us a little.

By this time, more people were traveling the road who were refugees.

We did not speak to those we did not know, especially those who spoke a different language, as this was the way we protected ourselves. But more and more there were old men and women of all ages and young children and many boys. There were a few girls our age, as there would always be in the camp, but there were many more boys. The group swelled as we walked. We kept to ourselves, but during the walk through the villages of the western Ethiopian countryside on our way to Itang, our numbers were about 300 people.

Occasionally, we would see someone sleeping by the side of the road, but we did not disturb them. We were very tired. If someone fell down, they fell to sleep right away, and snored immediately. We knew that person would not wake up, so we went and woke the person up, saying, "Let's go, you will get time to rest. You'll get to sleep."

I've been asked if we made up songs about food as we did about cows, or girls. It is the custom in my tribe to make up very elaborate songs about our cows, their color, their horns, and the sway of their walk. And our songs about a favorite girl and her attributes grow long and involved—practice for when we will sing to her in adolescence and begin the flirting and socializing that will eventually end in marriage. At the time of our marriage, there would be an exchange of our families' choice cows.

We don't sing in the same way about food, describing its flavors or colors or taste. There is a taboo about singing about food. In fact, in my culture, it is not polite to ask for food. To beg is to disgrace yourself. We are told that we will have enough. If we do not eat today, then we will have food tomorrow. We will always have enough.

I think it helps if other people know the way that we adapt; if they know what we do to deal with situations that threaten our lives, maybe they'll get some ideas of how to deal with bad things in their lives. For us in our culture, when we were with our grandparents, they had to teach us everything that is learned from generation to generation. My grandparents would say, "If something happens to us or to your parents you have to be patient, make yourself to be strong, God will help you, and you can be a better person in the future." The other thing that was impressive to me was my grandmother said, "If you are having problems, don't think about the food we give you here. If you think about it too much, you are going to die."

Food being such an important part of life, our grandparents and parents try to help us keep our expectations low so that we won't die because food has become so important. In fact, that training turned out to be the difference between life and death for many of us, as we found later at Pinyudo.

But on our long and difficult journey, we did wonder about why we were having to go so far, to walk in foreign lands, to even go to another country, just to find enough to eat, to be safe, and to be able to have future lives. Where was the world while we walked?

Here in Ethiopia, we continued our way of walking in the night, stopping after midnight, sleeping for four hours, then rising and walking until midday when we could rest for a few hours when the sun was hottest. In Sudan, we would look for a tree to rest under, but there were few trees here. And we were in Nuer country, so while we did not have to worry about the Sudanese Army, we had to watch out for enemy tribes and unfriendly villagers.

Then we were in an Anwok area. We gathered maize from stacks of stalks that were left in the field to dry. These particular people cut their corn stalks down with corn inside, and they piled the stalks together. They eventually would store them inside their village storage areas, but while all dried, they were in the fields, so as we walked at night, we took corn from these piles, stopping to boil it later.

During the day we came upon villages, about one a day, and here the houses were made of grass, including the roof, and they were on one level. They did not have homes like ours made with mud and bamboo where families slept up on the second level off the ground and animals were below. Their grass homes were more like our rainy season camps where we went to escape the high waters for several months a year.

There was one thing more that was different about this area. About the third day, we saw a mountain on the horizon. We had never seen this, and it caused quite a lot of talking back and forth about it. As we drew nearer, it grew bigger. When we arrived, finally, in Itang, the mountain seemed to loom over the camp. Later we found out it was another two hours from the camp.

Numbers of people had already gathered at Itang. There were old and young, men and women, and children, many children. There were UN-provided tents, and there was food. But it was also near a river, and it was wet and swampy. We had daily rations that included some staples, like wheat flour, maize, beans, oil, sugar and salt, but there was never enough. Powdered milk was also distributed, but if we drank too much of this, we suffered from bloating. People actually died after eating too much; it was called "suffocating stomach." One guy died—they kept us away from him. My uncle told me not to drink much of this.

We got used to sleeping at night—all the way through—and rising early in the morning. We had activities to help keep the camp, but there were not other organized games or competitions. It was rainy, and it stayed muddy a lot of the time. So while we had enough water, maybe we had too much.

At this point, as I look back, I see my life began to change in big ways. For one, our small group—Laat, Matoc, my uncle Dut, Kau, and I—were separated. After walking 500 to 600 miles over several months, we were no longer together. This was because soon after I arrived at Itang, I met an elder, Akec Rang. My uncle knew a friend of his. He was Dinka, but from the Cic Dinka tribe. Still, he had connection to our people because he had married a lady from the Agar Dinka tribe like mine.

"You are supposed to go to school," he told me. "At Itang you will not have anything." So, after I was at Itang for about a month, he paid for a car to take me and two others, Malual and Bec, to Pinyudo, where he said we could have school. He accompanied us there.

Before I left, my uncle Dut left Itang and walked to Pinyudo. Laat followed me to Pinyudo three weeks after I'd left. Matoc stayed in Itang, but I found him at Pinyudo later, in a different group from mine. My uncle would be in an adult group in Pinyudo, although I would not see him there very much.

What we saw first at Pinyudo was a large number of houses, more than the usual number in the villages we passed while walking. Then, further away from the houses, we came to an area where people were gathered and they seemed to be staying, not moving on. We then learned that this was Pinyudo, and there was to be a refugee camp here, but there were no signs this was a camp. There were no tents. People were just staying on the ground there.

The scene was very disorganized. The car left, and Akec left, and we were there, three boys who did not know each other well. We were Dinka, but we spoke different dialects. We sat on the ground there. We had shorts and shirts on. We were not naked, as there had been some food and clothes at Itang. Most of the other boys were naked. Many of the others were in rags.

More and more people arrived at the camp area. There were many languages. It was difficult to tell who was going to help us. There was no food, and there was no other support.

Finally after about a month, we were told to gather in certain areas, and they created several large groups: boys, girls, and then adults, including adults who had young children with them. We were considered "unaccompanied minors," as we had no adults with us. My uncle I could not see, but later I understood he was in a group with the adults.

As many as 300 people at a time came to the camp, but they could not stay together—the organizers wanted to mingle the tribes among themselves so that they would have better cooperation. This way we had to live with people who were not like us, but we learned to work out how we communicated and got tasks done.

Group leaders, many of whom later became our teachers, were selected to be in charge of each subgroup of minors. We were organized into groups based on our age. Among the unaccompanied minors, there were 12 groups, and I was in Group 9. Further designations were made so that each subgroup leader looked after 10 boys.

In this area there were more trees, and we camped under these. We did not have blankets, we did not have food, and there were snakes and scorpions to look out for. The young children were not able to survive that way—no food or blankets, and their stomachs were empty all the time.

By this time it was the rainy season, and we heard trucks of aid could not get through because of the deep mud caused by rains on roads from their headquarters in Gambela, Ethiopia. The aid was to come from the United Nations through its aid agency, the United Nations High Commissioner for Refugees (UNHCR). We were aware of UNHCR personnel in the camp from the beginning. Their compound was being constructed and they were erecting a big tent to distribute the food.

People in the camp began dying of starvation, or disease, or exposure. They had walked, like us, for hundreds of miles, through the desert and hostile lands where some were killed by native tribes afraid they were coming to take their territory. They'd run from areas where soldiers were, but some fell to soldiers' bullets when they went too close to a town. They'd escaped wild animal attacks, snakes, and poisonous bites. They kept walking without food and water until their feet were bloody. They'd lost companions, their families. Their hope was the refugee camps in Ethiopia. Now that they had arrived, it was safe, and they didn't have to walk; there were not soldiers or hostile people that would kill people.

But there was great hunger, there was no food, they were naked, and there weren't even blankets on which to lie on the ground.

Finally, a truck arrived, but by this time there were thousands of people lying or sitting under trees and all over the camp. Our large groups of unaccompanied minors were in one area, adults in another, but there were so many.

The one truck that got through came with 20 bags of corn or maize, but that cannot feed 15,000 children. It was really bad because when they came to distribute that corn, some people ended up with one kernel of corn and that's all the person had to eat. Now children were thinking about their mothers and how they served them with their food, thinking that if they were back home, they could get food anytime. So that is the reason people died—loss of hope.

This is the only reason I can think that I did not die. I remembered my grandmother's lesson from long ago: not to long for the food that she used to feed me and that my mother used to feed me. There was no food. People had to hope there would be food the next day. Many could not do that.

Many boys were dying because of lack of food, cold weather, and diseases. Many boys used to collect maize that dropped on the floor during distribution, and that's all they got. We were naked because UNHCR did not provide clothes. The young children were not able to survive under the trees without food and blankets. We lived under trees for six months, and in that time we lost more boys because of these lacks.

I remembered three boys who died at night because of starvation. It was one day that we had received a small amount of food in the distribution and some people decided to keep it for the following morning so they would have enough food until the next food arrived. When we woke up in the morning, the three had died while they slept. They had not eaten for two days and probably they'd had even less over the months. The UNHCR official came to see what happened to those children, and some of the other boys were selected to go and bury them. We used to bury our friends, and this was unjust to have a child bury another child at our age.

There was no regular food available for five to six months. In that time, hundreds of children died. The children also had malaria, malnourishment, diarrhea and dysentery. If you have some corn and you don't even boil it, and you have a long time not eating anything, it can have a reaction on your stomach. And if you drink a lot of water, that can also bring diarrhea. Diarrhea killed a lot of people. Also, chicken pox started coming out on the bodies. Nobody got immunizations when they were young, so those were the other things that people had.

We would go to the cemetery for the burial of a person in our group, and we would see another child we knew being buried. It seems like those burials happened every day.

Where was the world while this happened? Couldn't the UNHCR have acted faster to bring food and shelter to prevent the deaths of these children? They are supposed to be looking out for disasters like this, thousands and thousands of children and refugee families—couldn't the countries of the world have moved faster to help us? Those are questions I still have.

How did we deal with these desperate conditions? Older Sudanese refugees in the camp came up with the idea of organizing games and dances. There were dances for children that involved a series of moves like a couple of girls would dance and then they would select a boy to dance with them, and then two of those would dance together while the second girl would then select another partner. Other children clapped their hands to provide the music. Children took turns selecting each other as partners until everyone was dancing. These kinds of games and dances were entertaining.

I've mentioned before that there were many languages among all the people on the long walk to Ethiopia. In camp, this was true as well. We found people who could speak our language by hearing someone saying words we recognized. There was a connection, and we did things together. In Group 9, I found some others who spoke the same Agar Dinka language. Then, as we did on our journey, where we had different words for the same thing, we would agree on words we would all use in common to help us understand each other.

While these were necessary distractions, life continued to be hard in Pinyudo. One incident shows how just trying to provide for shelter had life-and-death consequences. I think there should have been a better way to watch over the many, many children in the camp and provide for their safety. This day ended up with some children becoming lost, and probably they died. We do not know.

At the time of this trip into the bush, it was six months after we arrived at Pinyudo. Food deliveries had become more regular. Some adult refugees were identified who could become our teachers. We were still sleeping under trees.

In our group, Group 9, we were ages six, seven, eight, and nine. Our group leaders and teachers had organized a trip to find our shelter and bedding material in the forest. We were told the night before that tomorrow we were going to find material for our houses and beds. We were excited because we didn't know how bad it was in the forest. In the morning we woke up early, at 4 a.m., and we went together before the others, proud to know that we were going to the forest first. We were about one thousand children that morning walking to find the materials—large sticks and grasses mostly. We stayed with everyone until 7 a.m., and then at 8 o'clock, we left the group, because we knew each other and we thought we could gather our materials together. By 10 o'clock we had all our grasses and sticks of wood. And then we tried to return back to the group, but we had lost our way back home.

We were lost for the whole day. We were trying to go back home early, but we just went deeper inside the dark forest. The big problem was that, because of tall grass, we could not see anything, no familiar natural markers, to help us find our way home. We climbed up on a tree to see if we could tell which way to go, but we couldn't. We were very thirsty because there was no water to drink for the whole day, not to mention no food.

From the trees around us came the frightened screeches of monkeys—calling to alarm other monkeys. This is the sound they make when there are wild animals around. I was very used to paying attention to animals' alarm sounds back in my home village. We had gone a long way from home—not one of the trees in that place had any cuts on them from humans taking limbs from trees. When we heard the cries of the monkeys, we made the decision immediately to go back and follow the way that we came from. After about a three-hour walk, we ended up getting back to camp that night at 9 p.m. We'd been gone on our own since 8 a.m. Teachers and group leaders were preparing to search for us in the morning, but we arrived safely, and everybody was happy to see us.

I keep remembering that day. I don't think I'll forget that hard day in my whole life. I still remember my three friends I went looking for grass and limbs with. Mangar Ayii was a Cic Dinka (the Cic live to the southeast near Bor, in South Sudan). I think he may have returned to his home. Yel Garang was a Malual Dinka; he is in Seattle, Washington. And Yai, another Malual Dinka boy, is in Texas. (The Malual Dinka are in the Bahr el Ghazal region of South Sudan, but much farther west than my home.)

We were sure that other children were not so lucky, that they did not return from that trip, because there was no adult making sure each group traveled and returned safely. That was another incident where we feel the camp organizers should have been more careful in preventing children from becoming lost and dying in the forest. I know there were some losses, as I had a cousin who was on that trip, and his friend who went with him was never found.

We made our houses out of sticks and mud, with a grass roof. The grasses also were used for our beds. All of us worked to build our own shelter. Once we did this, we also went out to gather grasses to build our classroom.

Just as the group leaders had come from the older Sudanese there in Pinyudo Refugee Camp, so did the idea for starting schools so that we could receive our education. We began classes under a tree in the camp, led by those older Sudanese who had received schooling themselves, and this soon led to constructing a classroom building.

This classroom was one large open building made of tree poles for support and a very big single roof made of grasses laid on pole framing and lashed down to secure it.

When we started having school, we used charcoal from our fires instead of chalk, and cardboard cut from the large boxes our cooking oil came in became a blackboard. The classes were really big. A teacher would teach 100 children in that large classroom building, and then we would go outside in circles and in small groups, we would each take turns writing "1" or "8" or our letters or whatever was the lesson. Later, they tried to give us sheets from exercise books, but there were not enough materials for each to have a booklet. They gave us an exercise sheet and we cut this in two. All pencils were broken in half to give to students. Sometimes in the group they would learn the material. But it was really slow.

I was going to school. At Pinyudo, I learned my numbers and letters and some basic math. This was the school information I wanted to learn. Back in our villages, only a few (one boy out of a family) would be spared the hard work of cattle grazing and farming. If the war had not come to my village, I would have eventually gone to school in Arabic, as the schools were supported by the Sudanese government, which is predominantly Arab and Muslim. What a different fate and schooling I had, there with 15,000 Sudanese children from all across southern Sudan, learning my letters in English by writing in the dirt with a stick. But I was glad to learn English and to have this be the start of my education, which was completed in those refugee camp schools.

This is what I was to do in my family, become educated. But my family was not with me. It was painful to think of being away from my family.

Laat, who was with me on my journey from southern Sudan, was in Group 3. I knew my uncle was in Pinyudo somewhere. There were other boys I was meeting, but I was missing my mother and my grandmother and my brothers and sister. Were they safe? Where were they? I didn't know these things. And in my group there were a thousand other boys who were wondering the same things about their families.

The dance became more important to me at this time. I was very popular as a partner for the pretty girls, and it felt good to be selected to dance. We performed dances called Ayelyom and Kelle. I was even selected to dance for the UNHCR officials when they visited Pinyudo Refugee Camp. It was a way to welcome the officials; it was fun and enjoyable for me. The dancing made me focus without thinking about my parents at that time. I thank my parents for their help to let me know how to dance our traditional dances. I did it for fun and to keep myself out of trouble thinking about my mother and my home. When I came back home from activities, I felt tired and I fell asleep immediately. I did not have time to think about home, or about those colleagues who had died or who had been lost on the hunt for shelter and bed materials.

Four

Seed of Sudan

For the first six months of our stay at Pinyudo Refugee Camp, we were plagued by a lack of food. It was one thing not to have food on our long journey when our enemies were also thirst, exposure, wild animals, and soldiers. It was quite different to be in a large camp, sheltered by homes we'd built ourselves of mud, sticks, and grass, row upon row of dwellings organized in subgroups of a thousand, 12 to 15,000 children in all, children suffering and dying for lack of food.

We arrived probably in late 1987, and that was a time of no food probably for a month until the first truck was finally able to get through. Children perishing from starvation and loss of hope, as well as illness, was a daily event. I will never forget this time. It was probably in May of 1988, six months later, that food started coming more regularly, but we still were limited to one meal a day. We ate no breakfast or lunch, but only dinner, and that was also very little, usually beans or corn, very little meat. The uncertainty of distributions made people hopeless. We in our group tried to encourage each other not to lose hope, just as we had on our journey.

Eventually, malaria began to attack some refugees. That was added to the problem of diarrhea, a continuing tragedy where people became dehydrated and died. Dysentery was a problem. There was also a disease caused by some meats. Dinka call it *agui* or *magui*. If you eat meat with this disease, it can kill you. If you eat it, you become very constipated and your eyes turn yellow and your urine is very yellow. Our people would use the local medicines, the local beer or *mou heer*, to cure it, but we did not have this. In 1988 or 1989, there was a Catholic Church that was opened in the refugee camp, and that church was served by sisters (nuns) from Italy, and they had a medicine that could treat this disease. So they treated people with *agui*, and that is when it was discovered there was a Catholic priest in the camp who was one of the refugees.

The Italian Catholics contacted their headquarters in Addis Ababa, Ethiopia, and they sent this priest's name to Addis and found out he had been ordained in 1982. They told the priest—his name was Father Madol—that they would get him a car so he could open a church for the people in the area around Pinyudo, and then he could help the people in the camp. As you'll see when my story continues, the priest was a great friend to the people in the camp, and having the Mass became very important to us as a way of praying for the many problems people had in the camps and for our families left behind in southern Sudan.

Before Father Madol was discovered, people would just pray under the tree. They would gather at a specific time and pray. Then Father started saying Mass under the tree, and that was good. After that, also, we began receiving medicine and clothing from Ethiopians in Addis Ababa. Finally, we had been discovered and our needs were becoming known, and someone else was helping us.

We had another distraction once some of the elders in the refugees helped organize soccer and volleyball games. Someone provided balls so we could play, and playgrounds were set up in each of the 12 groups. These games were new to many of us, especially to me, but I discovered I really liked volleyball, and I was good at it. Being tall for my age helped!

Once food did start to arrive, a system was set up where each group (there were about 1,000 boys in each group) would take responsibility for distributing and storing the food. We have 12 groups, and the 12 groups each have a playground where they can play soccer, volleyball or basketball. The UN brings the food from the store; they put it on the truck, and they bring it to the group. They put it in the playground, and then the group leader comes and tells the village leaders to get their food. And each group stores the food in one place. This is the ration for one month, and our leader portions it out. Then after a month, they have to get a new ration. So it was really easy. Anyone could see the food. The boys would see the food and know that it is there. Every group and subgroup of that larger group has its own food. There is a day, and everyone knows when it is, when food will be distributed to people.

This process reduced the fear of not having food. It was a simple but important way of assuring the boys that we were not without food. It would have to be used wisely so that the ration would last until the end of the month. But we knew if we did that, we would have enough food.

Gradually we began getting the things we needed to survive there in the Pinyudo Refugee Camp. Especially it was a great achievement for our teachers to organize thousands of minors and control them in peace. Their efforts kept the young boys and girls united from the time they arrived, and their influence continues even until now. We Lost Boys counsel each other, advise one another, comfort one another, even today—we are all brothers who came together during this civil war that tore Sudan apart. Through the school, sports, and cultural activities we grew closer and support each other as we live in homes together, or visit one another in cities where Lost Boys have gone, or visit in our home country.

One way those teachers helped us was through discipline. They taught us how to live in the world. When we were in Pinyudo, we were not allowed to go to the market. The market was a place where Ethiopians gathered to sell and buy goods; these were people who had moved close to the camp to fill some of the jobs that became available as a result of this huge center being built to care for tens of thousands of refugees. The Ethiopians living there not far from the refugee camp would display their goods on cloths on the ground, and many sales would be transacted among the people.

We were not allowed to go there without permission from the teacher. During school hours, there were not supposed to be any students in the market. We could get permission after school was over or if it was a weekend. But there was a teacher who was assigned to patrol the market and make sure we didn't go there without permission.

The name of this teacher was Mathou. All minors knew Mathou for what he did to us, and it was good discipline for success. There were things he would not like minors doing: smoking, drinking beer, stealing, or taking money from the sellers. It was important for him for us to avoid these things. I believe I did not know anything about how to live my life before I lived in Ethiopia. Most of the minors were at first hurt he did not allow us to go to the market. All of us now realize that he wanted to make sure we were successful in our lives. He used to tell us we were the future of Sudan. The image he was looking at for us minors was education to support our country in the future; that was why he kept people focused on school and studying.

Our teachers were treating us like the seed of Sudan's future. They did not feel good if any one of us did not obey the rules of education. They really trained us well beyond their ability. It was wonderful for these teachers to make changes in us that so that we can be leaders, fulfilling their dreams and ideas. I hope we are not going to let them down because they showed us the ways to struggle. Many minors of Sudan who went on to other places in the world should think about these people and how they influenced us. I believe some of our teachers are still in Kakuma refugee camp and they are teaching other children right now.

Since 2011, South Sudan has been independent from Sudan, and Lost Boys, whether in South Sudan or in other parts of the world, are doing an important job for their parents, relatives, families, friends and other Sudanese. They are heroes to children around the world who faced the hardship of the life during this civil war in Sudan. We are still struggling, because even after the peace agreement that ended the war, and after independence, there is much to do to make our new country strong. With our experiences of walking to find safety, adapting to new homes in several refugee camps, learning in school, learning the discipline of the right life from teachers such as Mathou, and later building new lives after leaving the camps, we are better prepared to contribute to this new future for South Sudan.

Sudan, and now South Sudan, face many challenges in the future. For many, many years, there has been a divide between the Sudanese government and southern Sudan. The problems can be expected to continue for many years to come. We Lost Boys were separated from our families at very young ages—many of us six, seven and eight years old— and many are still separated. We became orphans at early ages, and endured extreme hardship, all because of the war within our country. It is estimated that 2 million people died and many thousands were removed from one part of the country to the other and out of the country as a result of the war. We Lost Boys have seen the results of violence in our homeland. We are determined to create a peaceful, progressive future for our country.

Even though conditions at Pinyudo did improve, my impatience and curiosity grew; I wondered about whether there would be more food or resources back at Itang. I got permission to go back there to investigate for myself. I had learned on my long journey to keep going, to keep looking for resources, and I could not stop trying to get better conditions. I ended up staying for only a couple of weeks, for conditions there were not much different from Pinyudo.

In all our days at Pinyudo and Itang, there was a ray of hope, although we did not know the specifics of it. All we knew at the time there at the refugee camp is that someone important had died in a plane crash and he was on his way to see us. Later when we were in the United States we learned who he was. He was a U.S. congressman who'd heard of our plight, that civil war in southern Sudan had killed many, many people, and that thousands had had to flee to Ethiopia. His name was Mickey Leland; he was from Texas. He'd been to Ethiopia and Sudan looking into our camps, and he was trying to find a way for the United States to help.

Leland was on his way to Pinyudo Refugee Camp in 1989 when his plane crashed in the mountains of western Ethiopia. We were waiting for someone to come to see the problems. Imagine if Leland had come to Pinyudo and found the problems. We would have received some attention from America—America, the land with so many resources, so much freedom.

But no one came to find us. We still wondered where the rest of the world was in relieving the problems. It was not just our camps we were worried about, even though we never ate more than once a day, and there was illness, and much missing our families. We were concerned for our families and for our country in its long battle for resources that could help our lives; we needed help combating the Sudanese government, which took all our natural resources of water and oil, and provided no infrastructure, no electricity, no water systems. Now that government that gave us nothing was trying to kill all of us, and we needed other wealthy nations to come to our aid.

Where did the problems in Sudan come from? And what about Darfur? Many people have heard of Darfur. In fact, it is a sore point with the Lost Boys and the many others who suffered in southern Sudan that so many people were dying in the bombing and attacks on the villages in the south, and we were fleeing our homes, long before Darfur conflicts arose. Our civil war started in 1983, and the war extended past the time we eventually resettled in the United States in 2001. The war actually ended with the Peace Agreement in 2005. We believe the people in Darfur should be free of violence, also, but the problems of government attacks on their own people in southern Sudan began long before the world started hearing about Darfur, in 2003.

The native peoples of Sudan are those in south Sudan, Blue Nile province, Nuba Mountains, Darfur and other regions that are not Arab. Several centuries ago, the Arabs entered the Sudan area to trade with the native people in Sudan and west Africa. The traders then became those in power. A decision was made by the British to leave Sudan totally in the 1950s. Before that time they governed Sudan in an arrangement with Egypt. There was an attempt to separate the south from the rest of Sudan at that point, but southern Sudan agreed that they would stay with the Arab people and remain part of Sudan. A conference was held in Juba in 1950 with all chiefs of southern Sudan villages about separation of Sudan and they decided not to separate the southern provinces from the north. That was a mistake, as the Arab traders and their descendants, a people with a different religion and ethnic group from the natives, then ruled the country.

All the water from the headwaters of the Nile, which lie south of Sudan, is destined for Egypt. This is because Egypt and the Sudanese government determine these things, and the native people of Sudan do not have power to change things. All of Sudan's oil, most of which is in Bentui, Unity State—an area of southern Sudan—is pumped out and flows directly through the lower part of the country up to northern Sudan to Port Sudan on the Red Sea. All the revenues from the sale of oil go to the Sudanese government, which is controlled by Arabs. Egypt, whose development depends on waters from southern Sudan, does not appreciate how southern Sudan helps Egyptian people with water from the River Nile. Egypt supports their friends in north Sudan because of the Islamic Brotherhood.

These Arabs are Muslim. The people in the south are mostly Christian or animist, the native religion. The civil war in southern Sudan began over the attempt by the Sudanese government in Khartoum trying to impose the Muslim sharia law in all of Sudan. It began in 1983, and it reached my village in 1987. In time, some 80,000 refugees filled camps in Pinyudo and other locations. An estimated 2 million died in the war. Yet the news was not widespread about the civil war that eventually extended over two decades. Is it a coincidence that the United Nations Secretary during part of this time was from Egypt?

Khartoum focuses all the resources that it receives to develop the areas in the North rather than in the South and in other remote areas. There is no infrastructure—schools, hospitals, factories, roads, security— they are all lacking in southern Sudan, and before the civil war, the politicians from southern Sudan did not secure these things in their areas. Southern Sudan got two vice presidents before the civil war, but they did not build one house in their own home town. They lived in Khartoum for their whole life because they did not want to come back to southern Sudan.

Darfur is in western Sudan, and its characteristics are different from southern Sudan. In Darfur are many Africans who have over the centuries converted to Islam, but they are native Sudanese like those in the south, so they are Muslim Africans. It is important to know the truth, and that is that the Darfurians were the highest percentages in the Sudanese Army, the same army that killed many of our people in southern Sudan; it was those soldiers we were fleeing all those months on our journey, and the ones who would kill us if we did not reach safety.

At this time, the Darfurians regret what they did to southern Sudanese people, and we are still welcoming them as our people of one nation. We are all Sudanese. What happened in Darfur is that unlike southern Sudan, there are few natural resources in Darfur. There are no roads going into that area. Between Libya and Sudan, if you travel by car, you'll easily get lost because of dust. There's not any road you will see. Dust will cover it. In their area, it is desert; there are no resources, no water; their people rely on the government, and so when they started demanding resources, that's when the government started bombing their villages.

In our area, meaning the western part of southern Sudan where the Malual Dinka live, the Marleen, the nomadic sheepherders, came over into western Bahr el Ghazal, looking for water for their livestock. They took a lot of children from there, and that's why slave trading started. What affected us was the Sudanese government was not enforcing the border there. All through this region they took a lot of children and they killed a lot of people. Here is the Kirr River; they have to get water, so what happened was that during this dry season they come on this river; they burn all the houses around here and stay there, and they abduct the children and girls; then they kill the Malual Dinka's animals and get the meat, then take cows with them as they leave.

Back in Darfur, north of this area, the Janjaweed were given guns by the Sudanese government, so they warred on the native African tribes. They were also Muslim, but the government would set one part of the tribes against another, and they would say we will give you power, and then you can kill the other people. Those native people were wanting the government to provide them with health care and infrastructure and access to water. So then the Janjaweed, now armed, started warring on these Darfur Africans.

This all started long after our civil war had caused us to have to leave our homes, see our companions die, lose our parents and families—it had been going on since the early 80s. We were warred on earlier than Darfur, but the world heard more about Darfur, and it was termed "genocide." We feel the southern Sudan war was genocide as well. Likewise Rwanda, which experienced so many millions of deaths in 1994, was called genocide. Maybe these are called genocides because the rest of the world got to hear about them. After Rwanda, maybe the world was watching more. So those are the differences in the southern Sudanese civil war and the tragedies in Darfur.

Five

Fleeing Ethiopia

We Lost Boys of Sudan all had different experiences—we varied in age and came from numerous villages across southern Sudan when the civil war erupted, and journeys took different paths before we ended up in Pinyudo Refugee Camp. There were 12 groups that included about 15,000 boys altogether at Pinyudo. But we will all remember the Gilo River, and we will never forget that experience. If you ever meet a Lost Boy, you will know he is in fact a Lost Boy if you mention the Gilo River, and his reaction is to become either very quiet, or very angry, as he relates what took place.

First, we have to return to the country of our refuge, Ethiopia. During the Sudanese Civil War, the Sudanese government was determined to eliminate the Sudanese Peoples' Liberation Army, and the government's Sudanese Army held many of the southern Sudan towns. The SPLA, under the leadership of John Garang, fought for control from one village to another, attempting to take areas from the SA. The SPLA sanctuary was Ethiopia, and this safety was made possible because of the mutually helpful alliance between the dictator of Ethiopia, Mengistu Haile Mariam, and John Garang. Mengistu's protection made the camps able to operate eventually so that we could obtain food, shelter, and safety from the SPLA and the UN.

After the severe hunger of the first months in Pinyudo when so many children died, the food gradually became more predictable, although we continued to receive only one meal of corn or grain or beans a day. Still, we'd built our homes and a classroom. We'd found a priest among us, Father Madol, and we were having Mass, and we were about to begin construction of a nice church in our camp. There was a great deal of excitement about this. Life was a little bit okay for the unaccompanied minors at Pinyudo Refugee Camp.

Then, with the fury of a sudden desert dust storm, in May 1991, we were ordered to leave the country in 24 hours. After ruling Ethiopia for many years, Mengistu was overthrown by rebels, and the rebels ordered refugees to leave. In the camp, there was chaos. Where were we supposed to go? And how? People ran around in panic. All they could think about was the hard months of journeying to find safety, and how that now would start all over again.

There was no reliable transportation for us to leave the country. It was not a simple thing to do—there were no trucks to carry us or any other transport. Ethiopian rebels were combining their armies with Sudanese armies from the Khartoum government to take control of all of Ethiopia and to take revenge on the SPLA and its kind. We were going to be under attack anywhere we went.

Our leaders told us to run—and that's what we did. People had to try their best to walk by foot for 100 miles to reach the southern Sudanese border and, beyond that, the town of Pachala. Boys who had walked to Ethiopia through Pachala on the way to the refugee camps gave us directions.

We had to swim the Gilo River, a river forming the border with Sudan, in order to reach this safe area of Sudan. It was the rainy season, and the Gilo River was full of swift, turbulent water because of the heavy rainfall. People could not see the other side of the river, and they wondered how to cross. There were no boats or local fishermen to help them negotiate the river.

With my companions, I was able to swim in the swift water. There were high waves in the river. Coming behind us were the other refugees, and we were all trying to make it out of Ethiopia before the rebels caught up with us. We made it across, but others were not so lucky. In 1992, I talked to my friend Mawat who was there. The rebel troops came up behind those on the river's edge and began shooting; they forced people into the river with their heavy gunfire, and then continued shooting as people tried to swim across the river. If you were swimming in the river, three or four people jumped on top of you as they fled into the river. They bumped into bodies as they tried to cross. Others were killed by crocodiles in the river. So whether from being shot, or drowning, or being attacked by crocodiles, many, many people died at the Gilo River.[1]

Anti-aircraft were patrolling the borders between Ethiopia and Sudan and shooting at rebels who might be in those areas. They followed the routes to the towns they already knew, like Pachala. So the refugees avoided these places, moving beyond the river and Pachala to open fields outside the town. They had to go where they would not be hit by bombs.

The Ethiopian rebels themselves teamed up with the Sudanese government. They were actually based in Sudan. When the rebels overthrew Mengistu and we were told to leave for the sake of our lives, we walked away very quickly. I was one of the first, and since I was nearly 12 years old, and I'd grown tall, my natural tendency to move quickly was aided by long legs and moderately good health. That's why I could get to the river before most of the others who were caught up in the gunfire. There was a special group of refugees trailing far behind us that came out from Pinyudo, heading for the river. They could not walk easily because they were older, and there was an International Red Cross worker with them. When they got to Pachala, the Sudanese government bombed them. They captured them, including the IRC worker, and took them all to Khartoum. They released the IRC person, but they kept the children. I don't know what they did with them.

Those who were able to make it across the river then went further west, one hour from the Gilo, in Pachala. When people went to Pachala, there was no food. There is a small airstrip there; no planes carrying food could land there. The UN base at Lokichoiko, Kenya, was trying to figure out how to help the children. So they came out from Lokichoiko with flights, dropping food down on the ground there in Pachala. We were in an open expanse of land—few trees, no provision for cover. It took them a month to figure out how to fly in and make the food drops. It was the rainy season and people had nothing to eat. So when they started the flights, they dropped food down, and they killed some people with loads of food. While people were waiting for these food drops to get organized, they became so desperate they ate tree leaves, and a kind of fruit on the tree. There is a seed on the tree that people eat.

So we might get food from the airlift, but what about tomorrow or next month? There was no shelter, and we were wet a lot of the time from the rains. What kind of a life is that? This went on for several months.

As SPLA forces were now in control of some of the towns in the southern part of Sudan, camps were being set up to receive us. This is what we heard.

As the dry season began, in January, February, and March, we began moving south. We were encouraged to move toward the Kenyan border, as Sudan was still in civil war, and while the SPLA forces now controlled some of the towns, that could change. If the attacks became more threatening, we were closer to Kenya than Uganda, so we tried to go in that direction. We walked in large groups, moving toward Kapoeta, further southwest in Sudan, in Eastern Equatoria region. (It is now Eastern Equatoria state.)

This time, there were UNHCR support trucks that offered food and water to those walking, and a ride for a while for those who needed to rest. Belongings packed on our heads, we moved through Kapoeta, and then settled east of the town in an area known as Narus close to the Kenyan border. Again, we tried to stay away from population centers, as these could be bombed.

In Pinyudo, we had 12 groups. Then we had six groups within the same area, so we had a total of 18 groups. When people moved out from Pinyudo, they went back to their original 12 groups in these new camps. At Narus, refugees came out of the refugee camp in Ethiopia called Dima. These were more Sudanese. We were all unaccompanied minors, but now our groups included some that had not been at Pinyudo.

With all the movement and the addition of new people, it was hard to tell who had survived the Gilo River. There were other hardships along the way, as there had been in the loss of people while we hunted for grasses to build our huts at Pinyudo. Some people were missing, but some people may have been with different groups. Some may have gone back to their original groups, or they may have gone home to their villages. Years later, people pop up and you see them in passing, and you say, "You are still alive. I did not know that you were alive." But a lot of people, they are actually gone.

I wondered about my uncle who accompanied me to Ethiopia during my long time at Pinyudo Refugee Camp, and after. I rarely saw him at Pinyudo, and I did not know what group he was in. Only later did I find out that after Pinyudo Refugee Camp collapsed, he ran with all the others, but he walked home to find our village of Adut Maguen. He found the family at Pulkar instead. So my guardian on the way to Ethiopia is still living with relatives near the village where I was born, and I have seen him on my returns to our home. Kau also ran; he lives in Rumbek.

People had begun building homes in the Narus camp when all of a sudden, again, calamity struck. The Sudanese Army captured Kapoeta, and we had to move again. The attack came in the morning; in the afternoon, we were told to leave, to walk to Kenya, to Lokichoiko, where there was a UN base. We did not ask why, we just walked. We began walking at 6 p.m. and we walked all night. If we stopped to rest, we would not make it. Our group arrived at the Kenyan border the next morning, and we walked farther on to Lokichoiko.

Loki—we call it that—became our next stop. Set up on a wide expanse of flat land like our open fields in Pachala, this was not actually the town of Lokichoiko; it was outside the town close to the airport and to the Sudan border. So we just cleared bushes out and people slept on the plastic we put down.

Here the terrain was barren. There was no river, as there had been at Pinyudo. There we'd been able to swim in the river, and we had water not very far from the camp. In Loki, and later at Kakuma, both in northern Kenya, we depended on wells, because this area was very dry with hardly any rain.

It was at Loki that I was shocked at seeing our precious drinking water supply dirtied by a UN camp manager. I can only describe what I saw. When we arrived in Loki, there was a water tank that UNHCR had provided for refugees for drinking, cooking, and showering. The water was regularly pumped from the well, and stored in a large plastic container, kind of like a swimming pool with a cover that holds water collecting on the top. One day I was going to get some water from the water tank. The field official of UNHCR, a man called Phillip, was standing on the water tank. I remember when I saw him, I was very surprised, because I saw him as an official, and here he looked like one of us. He stood on the tank, and proceeded to use shampoo soap on his hair and then to rinse his head in that water. I left that day without getting water for me to drink, cook or shower. It took me two weeks to drink from the water tank again at Loki. This thing was very painful for me to talk about. Sometimes, it seemed the people who were to protect us did not care about us.

Refugees' leaders were reporting incidents to higher authorities in UNHCR to send Phillip away from the camp in Loki (there were other examples of mistreatment from Phillip), but UNHCR had failed to solve that problem. This was one of many events. UNHCR employees often treated people badly in my presence; we were considered like animals by some UNHCR officials, especially field officers. The water incident was something UNHCR personnel did that affected thousands of refugees.

Phillip eventually was killed in a Somalian refugee camp in northeastern Kenya, so perhaps he carried his disrespectful ways too far.

What bothered us in these cases where we experienced neglect or other actions that hurt us as refugees in the camp is that we see ourselves as people worthy of respect. The fact that we found ourselves in need and without a country was not our fault; we were people, just like the camp administrators. It seems that those who are refugees have few rights; what we receive in aid we are supposed to be grateful for and not to complain. Yet these kinds of actions can be helped if the UNHCR would make sure they employ only effective managers, not those who disrespect and abuse others in their care.

While we were in Loki, our next location, Kakuma, was not even a camp yet. It was started during the time we arrived at Loki; that's when the UN and the other agencies that were assisting them, such as Lutheran World Federation, were debating where they could put us. During this time, we also had the adult camps and the families' camp, so there were many, many refugees. We were there in Loki for two and a half or three months.

I turned 12 years old in 1992, in Loki, and a camp was under construction in Kakuma, further southeast in Kenya. They were cutting the trees to make the poles that would become the frame for our homes. They would have plastic for roofs. They also were laying out roads and determining the size of the groups, and then creating roads that could pass through these areas. They set up zones throughout the camp so that they could have a way of identifying and organizing all the groups. Now there were many more groups and so they were reorganized and renumbered.

We traveled to Kakuma by truck. And for the first time, the road was paved, a new experience for me—it was just like all the streets we see in Georgia now: all paved. Groups of us stood in the bed of the truck for the journey. In fact, the whole process of moving these thousands of people took two or three months. The day we got to Kakuma, people had been arriving for three days, and the camp directors were showing us where to set up. When we arrived, we were told to sit on the ground so that we could then be directed where to go. I rode in a truck with people from Rumbek—in fact one was a relative, an uncle, and there was a mother with two girls—and then I joined a group of unaccompanied minors as it was being assigned a place to camp. The UNHCR person did not have many skills in helping people get settled—in fact, he seemed to want to start a conflict among the groups he was dealing with. Two groups, Group 9 and Group 18, were assigned the same space. It was not large enough, and it contained a small creek. Since it was rainy season, a lot of the space was muddy, so there was not much area to set up camp. And then that one leader of Group 18, who was also a teacher, went and asked the UN guy and said, "You know, this space is not going to accommodate us. If you could take us to a different place, that would be good." The UN guy told him, "I am not going to do anything, so you can just go and stay. Or you can fight to see who can get another space."

So that group leader said he was not going to do that, he would just move his people to a different place. So that settled the problem. In the morning, he moved his people to an area that was not technically his; instead of staying in Zone 1, he moved to Zone 2. He did not want to fight with another group, but the UN guy seemed to want him to fight as a way to solve a problem.

This same camp director got in trouble with the Catholic priest, Father Benjamin Madol Akot. The field officer ordered Father Madol to move his church to a different place, and Father told him that this was a place he wanted to build his church, in the center of the camp. But the field officer would not let him build his church there. Father refused to leave the place he ordered him from; the field officer told Father that he was going to send him back to Sudan. The two of them got into a fight and they had to call Kenyan police to come and break up the fight. The field officer was fired immediately.

After these opening events, things eventually started happening for the good. We lived with the others in our group, with each group numbering about a thousand. Each of us was assigned to a house, and three or four people were to live in that house. They called our names and they told us where we could build our house, and they gave us poles and plastic and nails. Then they actually hired Kenyans to come in and make the house. They scheduled it so they would come to the group and they would demarcate everything, and then they would start building. So for the first time, we had someone providing a home; we did not have to gather sticks and make mud and create our own walls.

At least that was the way it was for a while. Then the plastic that was being used for roofing melted in the sun. We complained to the UN people and they said they would survey, but this was complicated. The people who were in charge of construction for refugees would take some time before coming to survey. And it would take some months for them to build your house or secure the material for you, so people got tired of it and said, "Give me some materials, and I can do it myself."

Unlike Pinyudo, there were no grasses in this area, and there was no tree you could see the leaves on. In fact, I think they went out of the area to West Pakot in central Kenya to get the trees for the poles they supplied. The UN would even deliver firewood to us. We could not go and get anything. The local people around here could shoot us, we were told. In Ethiopia, we could go anywhere, get the trees and build our houses, and there's a lot of grass and plenty of grains. However, this area of Lokichoiko and Kakuma was a desert with none of these resources.

So we requested materials from the UN camp managers, and some people they did give material to and some not. We started installing *macute*—palm leaves stitched together—to make the roof. Walls are formed of upright sticks, and then you place the mud on top of that. That was the solution we refugees came up with.

Because of the UNHCR, Lutheran World Federation, and many other aid agencies, Kakuma Refuge Camp was a very good place in 1992 to 1995 for having food, water, and healthy conditions. People got a full ration for two meals a day, and water was available to drink, to cook, and to get a shower. The kind of food that we received at that time was wheat flour, maize or corn, sorghum, dry fish, cabbages, sugar, oil, beans and salt. These foods were distributed to everyone throughout the camp. Again, the food was brought to the groups, the group leader distributed it to all the boys, and the boys made it last through the week. The refugees' life was a little better during that period of time. In the middle of this period, about 1993, the Lutheran World Federation cut some of the food from the refugees' budget, so we no longer had wheat flour, dry fish, or cabbages.

In this camp there was a lot more order, and roads were in place to bring rations to each group and otherwise provide for walking among the groups. The camp grew rapidly. There was a terrible genocide in Rwanda in 1994, and we started having more Rwandans, and then, eventually, Somalis who were displaced by the collapse of civil government in that country came to Kakuma from refugee centers closer to Somalia.

The camp had more resources available than any of the ones we'd been in so far, and we were assured we were safe here, as we were far away from the civil war in Sudan. Yet people wanted to know when the war would end. No refugee camp is like being at home, and our group members and all the children in the camp wanted their families, or to know if their families were still alive. We were told the UN would support us from primary grades through Form 4, and they would provide that education. (In Kenya, as in many former British colonies, high school consists of Form 1, 2, 3, and 4. These are similar to grades 9, 10, 11 and 12 in U.S. high schools.) After that we would be released. Where would we work? Probably we wouldn't go to a university, as Kenyans didn't like us, and weren't likely to have us attend, even if we qualified.

So here we were in Kenya, hopefully safe, looking forward to being educated, but in a country where we were strangers, sometimes barely tolerated, a situation we encountered over most of the 15 years of our journey.

Six

Kakuma Refugee Camp

Many times in our travels to other countries outside of Africa, we've found confusion about our country—some people think Sudan is Somalia, or vice versa, possibly because both start with the letter "S." And people don't know the culture of, say, Kenya versus Sudan, or how West African countries may differ from East African. Each country really has its own culture, and there are often many different tribal cultures within a single country, just as in southern Sudan, there are Dinka, Nuer, Murle, and quite a few others—and a hundred languages.

The culture of Sudan is very, very old, as it is in these other countries. There are many strong tribal influences, and there are religions and government forms that have been introduced, especially during the colonial period, which is really late when compared with the cultures in these African countries. In the late 1800s through the mid–1950s and '60s, European nations competed with each other to see who could own the most of Africa. Britain shared control of Sudan with Egypt from the end of the 1800s until 1956, and then Sudan became independent. British culture influenced Sudan, but not to the extent that British colonial rule affected Kenya and quite a few other countries. Sudan did see introduction of Christianity to southern Sudan, and to this day, the conflict between the Christian/animist culture with the Islamic culture of northern Sudan—its native African culture gave way to Islam, the faith of Arabs moving into the area in the 1500s—continues to color Sudan's history. Some of Sudan is Muslim; the Muslim Africans of Darfur represent a second culture, but among the Lost Boys and the southern Sudan area, the

66

tribespeople are primarily Christian or traditional African religion. Kenya is predominantly Christian. Somalia, however, is predominantly Muslim; its northern tip is directly across from the Arabian Peninsula, and it traded directly with Islamic countries over the centuries.

There are conflicts within these countries between minority and majority populations; in Sudan, the presence of many different tribes presents opportunity for conflict, although most disputes are localized and involve scarcity of resources. Unlike European and Western countries, there is not a lot of infrastructure, no water systems, electricity, good roads and schools, and no strong government structure seeing to the needs of the population. In fact, tribal areas move, sometimes with the season, sometimes with internal wars. Borders are often a compromise after a conflict, and disputes can recur, changing these demarcations.

The one thing we knew in our travels and what we still know today: We tread carefully wherever we go, because conflict with strange groups is frequent in our area, due to these many tribal groups as well as conflicts introduced historically by the non-native ethnic groups coming into our midst. It's like walking on eggshells: We try not to break anything, but sometimes it is inevitable. On our long journey from Sudan to Ethiopia, back to Sudan, and then to Kenya, we learned we had to know when to leave a place we had just entered.

On our journey, each village we came to, we realized what we faced up ahead: maybe help, maybe trouble. Often people would offer us some food, but because they had family and villagers to provide for, we could not stay long. They might put some meal in a gourd for us, and we had to take nibbles of this as we continued our walking.

Why would villagers not welcome us? They would suspect that we were not just there for relief, but instead wanted to move in and settle there, and that scared them. They had land enough for their needs, but if others came after us and our families followed, there would not be enough.

I believe our journey offers a lesson in how our problems in Sudan, in Africa, and other parts of the world will be solved in the long run: One village at a time, one settlement at a time, we will learn how to get along with each other. First, it will take approaching carefully, respectfully, and knowing what the other person's needs are, and the boundaries we need to observe. Within that, not trying to impose our culture on theirs, we need to find the areas where we can agree we need to help each other, just as we did in making shoes and pots and pans for the people in Poktub in our first journey east through southern Sudan.

We relied on each other, and we still rely on each other, in making decisions about our future moves, whether in Clarkston, Georgia, Nashville, California, or Syracuse, New York. This practice of consulting each other comes from our Dinka culture. We are used to our elders negotiating important decisions for the family and for the village. We relied on our parents and grandparents to set guidelines for us. We retain the reliance on elders—I'll write soon about Lutheran Ministries of Georgia, Mama Gini Eagen, and the many, many people who assisted with our transition in Clarkston. Respect for elders is a characteristic of our culture.

Just as my uncle persuaded me that first day on the run from our flaming village to wear my gourd to carry precious water, we try to use discussion and logic to help each other when confronted with a problem. Our parents taught us many skills to help us on our journey, especially how to help ourselves when no one else could give us aid. It's a lesson we keep applying today.

So here we were in Kenya; all was not perfect, but we adapted. If the local Turkana people did not like us, and we could not go outside the camp, we would do something else. What we did was sports.

Our sports training and competitions had started in Pinyudo. There was an adult refugee, Madong Mading Ater, who was from Rumbek near my home village, and he was very skilled in all sports. He taught us soccer, volleyball, and basketball, and organized many teams within the camps, and in the zones. He was in charge of the sports in the camp at Pinyudo and also at Kakuma, so he set up a lot of competitions. At Kakuma, he also arranged handball, and I don't know what other sports he did. For soccer, volleyball and basketball, we even had the zone teams select the members of Central teams that would play teams outside the camp, competing against Itang or Kakuma area teams. In addition, there were athletics, running competitions that were organized for the camp residents.

There were other teachers who knew how to play soccer and volleyball and basketball, because when things were good in Sudan, they learned all of these. Those people were assigned to train us in team sports. These teams were real active.

I became a very good volleyball player. I am tall, and this offers an advantage in spiking the ball or passing back and forth across the net. I was on the Central Team for Kakuma Refugee Camp, the Sudanese Central Volleyball Team; in fact, I was the team captain. In addition, I played

Majok (standing at left) at Rumbek reunion with coach and mentor from refugee camps, Madong Mading, with his wives.

basketball. All these sports were new to me, as was soccer, for when I was growing up in the bush, we played with homemade balls made with the sap of local plants, and we had games we played, but we did not have organized athletics.

I was also a coach of volleyball for Zone 2 of the Kakuma Refugee Camp; I trained many boys and girls in volleyball from 1996 to 2001. All this was volunteer work. We won a lot of trophies. Among others, we played against church soccer, basketball, and volleyball teams. We won a lot of cups from them. We played in a church league, and our Catholic church we attended in Kakuma camp was called Holy Cross. When a tournament was being arranged, people at the opponents' churches would ask, "Is Holy Cross going to come?" They knew we were tough competition. So we got volleyball cups all the time.

All these athletic competitions helped because when people came back from school, they had to go to practice, so it made it easier for everyone. When they were working like that, they couldn't be thinking about their problems.

In school, we had full exercise books; we didn't have to cut the pages of a book to share. The UN distributed the exercise book, and pencil or pen. If your pen ran out of ink, you had to buy your own. If we needed a pen, we would trade a half-ration for money to buy a pen. That meant we were really hungry for the next week.

The food was still being brought to the group. They left it there, and you used your ration card to get your cup of grain. It would have to last for seven days. They give you beans, salt and oil. Later, they had to cut the oil. But we were in charge of our own ration, at least at that time.

I've been asked if people attempted to take food from each other. That didn't happen. If you steal food, that puts a mark on you. If you were Dinka, you did not do that. You would be seen as weak if you did that. So those things are tied to the culture. You would just say "I'm not going to die; I'll get my ration tomorrow." When this happened, you just made up your mind you were not starving. You just went inside yourself. You said this was just something that happened to you.

During this period, 1992 to 1995, the stress of having such a large camp (it eventually grew to 80,000) was affecting the local tribe, the Turkana. In each area so many refugees present in an area restricted where people could graze cattle, and that is what they live on. Pasturing their cattle, moving them from one very dry area to another to find enough grass, was their main occupation. Having routes and resources restricted made them angry. The Turkana had many, many guns and they began shooting into the camp, and in this period, nine refugees were killed by gunshots fired during the day. And in 1997, an Episcopal priest was killed in the camp at night by a local tribesman's bullet.

Father was killed about a half mile from where I lived in Kakuma. It was a terrible thing to go in the morning and see his body lying in the camp where he fell. It was destructive for the whole camp to face the fact that someone hated us so much that they would kill the priest, our Father. There were many times when the harshness of the refugee life affected me very deeply, and this was one of those times. All I could figure out is that I could not do anything about these problems; God had plans for me. The civil war in Sudan started during my generation, so it was God's plan to live that way, to move from country to country all my young life, but it was not an easy thing to do as a human being, for me or for my colleagues. I believe God created the children of Sudan to do something to change our country, which is now South Sudan. I love my country so much, and I hope we Lost Boys are going to do something significant to change life for our people in South Sudan. I am not going to forget my hard life in the refugee camp with my fellow refugees.

The last thing that I wanted to do was give up. I had seen colleagues die by the wayside on the journey to Ethiopia and watched children perish at Pinyudo from lack of hope. I'd known people to disappear, and knew many lost their lives at the Gilo River. My instinct all along the way was to keep walking. Now I could not walk out of Kakuma, but I needed to use every resource to focus on how to survive the pain of these deaths.

Fortunately, still another distraction emerged in the form of community dances in Kakuma Refugee Camp. When I was at Pinyudo, we performed children's dances. Now that I was older, I could learn and take part in the traditional male dances of the Agar Dinka. In the Rumbek area, where Agar Dinka are predominant, we are famous for our jumping in our dances. If you go online to You Tube and search for "Rumbek Dancing and Jumping," you will find examples of the kind of dances we do. Traditionally, the men are in the middle, the women on the sides, but the women have their own dances as well, and they are very good.

At Kakuma, we would meet in community; Rumbek area, or Agar Dinka people, would meet and dance, older people and younger, from different groups in the camp. Since I was not in my home village, I did not undergo initiation. That is the painful traditional scarring of the forehead, six incisions made across the forehead, by which an Agar Dinka shows he is able to withstand pain without complaint and thus signals he is entering manhood. In the camp we did not do these rituals. Because we were not in our home villages, we did not extract the lower teeth in the mouth at this time.

Instead, my entry into manhood was enduring all the hardships we encountered in our long search for our safe home. Because I was now of age, in our camp I could participate in the dances that symbolized entrance into manhood, including the dancing and jumping that are unique to our tribe. I became quite good at it, as I could jump really high.

In the evenings sometimes there would be dance competitions among dancers in the communities. On Refugees' Day, June 20, all the different tribes would do their dances—Dinka, Nuer, Murle. We would also do this on American Labor Day in September. Our dance style is very exuberant and joyful, and the refugees loved to see it. We have a lot of fun with our dance. So this was another way that I felt better and forgot about the difficulties of my life. After all, I was alive, and I did survive the civil war up to that point. I had many friends, and I was learning about my Dinka life and how it compared with other tribes and other people. I was very proud to be Agar Dinka from Rumbek area.

In 1993, the UN built the classrooms and school resumed for us. I went to third grade in the Juba Primary School. Eventually, in 1996, I would complete Grade 8 and sit for the Kenya Certificate for this in 1996. As time went on, I completed Form 1 (equivalent to the U.S. Grade 9), Form 2 (Grade 10), Form 3 (Grade 11), and Form 4 (Grade 12). All of this was in Kakuma Refugee Camp.

Food Fights

In 1994, a big problem at Kakuma arose from the food supplies. We got rations of grain—like a cup of grain to last us a week, perhaps with oil and salt. No longer were beans distributed. It was barely enough to survive on, and we had to be careful to stretch what was there in order to have food two times a day. Any change to this was a major issue.

Instead of serving regular wheat in our ration, a grain was substituted which was not edible. It was called *miath*, and another name for it was finger millet. In my village, it was recognized that it was so poor a grain, that it was used for fermenting into a beer instead of being cooked for food. The grains were very, very small. The effect of providing this in the diet is that it stopped up the digestive tracts of those who ate it, and could even lead to death.

A doctor who was one of the refugees went to the groups to see how they were cooking it. He was seeing people in the clinic they had there, and children were not being able to go to the bathroom for two to three days. He said they would die if they kept this up. He complained to the camp managers, but the servings went on for months and months. Meanwhile children were seriously affected by the food. This was not a case of staying out of school on purpose. The children in the camp wanted to learn; this was their way to have a better life. The situation went on for eight months, and everyone was suffering. Many people went to the UN compound to get the ration changed, but nothing happened.

The refugees finally started a protest. We blocked the road and would not let any UN vehicles in except those carrying the water people. Every morning from 7 to 9 a.m. they ran the pumps to fill the tanks (remember there are no rivers in this area, no sources of water); they also opened the pumps from 3 to 5 p.m. and the refugees and the UN compound had no other source for water in this desert area.

After a short time the UN asked for a delegate to visit the compound and they worked out a solution. The situation changed, and wheat grain replaced the *miath*. We did not know why the *miath* was substituted, only that it caused a great deal of illness. We did know that the camp was growing—quickly. In this time, there were about 50,000 people in the camp, and there were 53 groups of Sudanese. Of these, there were 17 groups of boys. In addition there were community groups of 18- to 50-year-old people gathered in their tribal and national groups. Among the refugees were Sudanese, Burundis, and Somalians. In addition there were people who wanted to form communities around their faiths. There was a Holy Cross Catholic Church community group, and there was an Episcopal Church community group.

From 1996 to 1999, the camp became even bigger. They had to build a larger distribution center. This was probably to accommodate large numbers of Rwandan refugees, as well as even more refugees from Somalia, as these increased the numbers at Kakuma in 1996. Now the camp held 80,000 or more.

The biggest change for us was that we had to each go get our food, and it resulted in extreme mistreatment from Kenyan police. The first sign of change was Kenyan workers employed by the UN building a huge metal wire fence around the new center. Within the outside fences, they built little columns, narrow paths bending back and forth so that refugees would queue up in these lines for food, rather than have food brought to their groups where the group leaders could distribute it.

The first day that they tried to have the refugees line up in this way for a bi-weekly ration, there was trouble. The Kenyan police were the ones who were directing the lines. When people did not move fast enough or objected to the long lines, police beat them with a stick. These police beat and beat those who were their targets. They struck on the joints—elbows and knees especially—where the pain is the greatest. I will never forget these scenes of beatings by the local police, who were hired by the UN to do this.

In terms of food, it was no different in amount. But when we had control of our own food, it felt more secure. As refugees, this was all we had. If I volunteered and coached volleyball for years, I received no pay. Like anyone else, all I had was this ration every two weeks. If I broke a pen or it ran out of ink, I traded half a cup of wheat—half of my food for two weeks—to replace it. Food was our currency, and we wanted to control that currency. To know we would not starve was very important.

But this food fight we did not win. We were forced into the fences, to stand in line for hours and hours for a single ration. In fact, I had to choose whether to eat or to go to school. If I stood in line, sometimes it would take two days to receive a ration. I had to be absent from school all that time, and I missed lessons that I needed to understand later information.

The Kenyan police carried this stick called a *rugu*, a Kiswahili word. They beat people even when there was no reason. They beat people like animals. Even though the UN saw that the police were beating them to a very dangerous point, nobody would say, "These are the people, don't do that." So it was a really bad life. Those blows to the joints would hurt for days.

There were some occasions when we traveled back to Loki for short visits. There was a checkpoint on the way; the cops would be up there. You would travel by bus, or *matatu*, a minivan that runs from Loki to Kakuma and from Kakuma to Lodwar. If you are in this area, and they see you are Sudanese, knowing you don't know Kiswahili, they would put you in this house they have and tell you that you have to provide travel papers, or you have to give them money. If you don't have the money, they put you in jail. I had found myself some papers, but I still had to give them money. That time was really bad.

The police, like other Kenyans, were thinking we were a people who do not have a country or do not have a good place. But if you go to South Sudan now, there are Kenyans everywhere. They have learned about our country and found it has many things to like. When we were in their country, they looked at us like we were not human. And they said we were bad people. We tell them, "You know what—we stayed in your country for nine years, and so we know what Kenya is like. We are physically very close to you, yet we didn't know what Kenya was like, and Kenyans didn't know what South Sudan is like. Now you see our country is not even like your country; we've got a lot of resources, a great deal more than in northwestern Kenya, and we have a good country."

In Kakuma, thanks to Father Madol and thanks to the large Catholic population in the town of Kakuma, we had a big Mass under the tree, and the Catholic people in the town supplied other needs to the refugees. They even sent people to lots of competitions like choir competitions. The Episcopal Church was also very big there. The choirs would compete.

They would go to Lodwar, the headquarters of the Turkana District, and they would be part of the competitions. This is where they also had leagues to play soccer and basketball and volleyball, and since I was coach of volleyball for Zone 2, I went on many of these trips.

The people we met there would say, "Why don't you people have a good country? People are fighting there, and you are competing with us?"

And we'd say, "Well, what do you do? It doesn't mean that if people are fighting in Sudan we don't do other activities." They thought that we would not have any talents to show other people, that we were coming from the bush and had no special skills. But we won a lot of volleyball championship cups from them.

Seven

Change Is in the Air

This change in how we got our food was traumatic to some people. The presence of the Kenyan police was more evident—they were everywhere. By this time, the camp had grown to more than 80,000, and included many Somalians who'd been moved from two camps in northeastern Kenya where there was a lot of violence. For those in the camp, the process of getting food meant not going to school. Since we had traveled so many miles over so many years to get to safety to have a future while southern Sudan was under assault, we were pretty unhappy with this situation.

Majok Marier (left) and Stephen Chol Bayok, friends since the Pinyudo Refugee Camp.

At the same time we knew there were not many alternatives. The war still raged in southern Sudan, and we knew from our forced exit from Pinyudo and the sudden move from Kapoeta that returning to the war zone was fraught with dangers. We did not hear much current news of the war, but we knew that there were no prospects for ending it anytime soon. This was in 1996; the war had begun in 1983. So there wasn't much hope we could go back home.

The coordinated protest to challenge serving the *miath* instead of an edible grain gave us a sense of ourselves as a strong force for change. We were not able to take part in the war, but we could strengthen ourselves in the camp. One way we did this was through our community meetings. Here everyone spoke Dinka, and so we could talk easily about what we knew of the war, and about other things.

If it was a perfectly dark night and I could not see the person when I heard it, I would still know another Agar Dinka by the sound of the voice. The way the person speaks would tell me, even if I could not see the person's height—we are a very tall people—or other physical markings. That is how I identified my friend, another Lost Boy, Stephen Chol Bayok.

—◊—

STEPHEN'S STORY
by Stephen Chol Bayok

I am one of the Lost Boys of Sudan. The name refers to survivors of the longest war in African history that caused many of us to walk hundreds of miles to three different countries seeking refuge. Many of us resettled in the United States in 2001. The civil war broke out in 1983 between the south Sudanese, who are Christian, and north Sudanese, who are Muslim. Most people around the world see it as civil war, but in fact, it was a religious war. Because it was the religious war, Darfurans who are African and Muslim in western Sudan, joined Arabic north Sudanese who are Muslim to fight their African brothers in the south. The Muslims in Sudan wanted the entire nation to be Muslims.

The Causes of the Civil War in Sudan

The most important factors that caused civil war in Sudan are religion, race, power and language. Within these factors, the most important factor that leads to civil war in Sudan is religion. Muslims in northern Sudan want Islam to be the national religion. For example, the government of Sudan was under the control of the National Islamic Front (NIF) until the Comprehensive Peace Agreement of 2005 ending the civil war was signed between north and south. This NIF government was the signal that determined the entire nation should be an Islamic nation. However, Christians in southern Sudan did not want a national religion, but instead they wanted freedom of religion. From the 1950s to 1987, Muslims in north Sudan tried very hard to convert Christians and other believers to Islam. For example, Muslims must be given a job before a Christian, and the Muslims do this successfully by tracing names such as Stephen, John, and so on. The Islamic Government used this job discrimination in order to convert the Christians to Islam.

Another more important factor which led to the war is power. Muslims do not want Christians to lead them because most of them believe that Christians are pagan and that nonbelievers should not rule them. Another is race. African descendants live in southern Sudan whereas Arab descendants live in northern Sudan. Each race sees the other race as less important in the country in term of cultures and traditions. There are two different cultures and traditions in the country. For instance, Arabs marry their cousins but Africans do not. Another less important factor, which leads to civil war in Sudan, is language. Arabs in Sudan speak Arabic but Africans speak their own languages, dialects, and English. Arabs want Arabic to be the main language in Sudan but Africans want to use all languages.

The Start of the War between the South and North

The government of Sudan passed sharia laws as the nation's supreme laws of the land in 1982 due to the pressure they received from the Islamic nations which support the government financially and militarily, such as Iraq. These sharia laws would have been applied to both Christians in the south and Muslims in the north. South Sudanese did not want sharia law to be applied in the south because sharia law dishonored Christian values. Sharia laws have more disadvantages then advantages. For instance, sharia laws say if a person steals something, their hand should be cut off; if a woman commits adultery, she should be stoned to death. This application of sharia laws to the entire nation and failure of the government of [Ja'afer] Nimeiri to implement the requests of Anyana One, the first civil war, in agreements in Addis Ababa in 1972 that ended the first war, fueled the second civil war.

Without alternatives for south Sudan, they formed the rebel group called the Sudan People's Liberation Army/Movement (SPLA/M) and started the war in nineteen eighty-three. The SPLA/M captured many towns in the south from 1984 to 1986.

The Government's Solution to the Civil War

Because the SPLA/M was very successful on the battlefield, the government's solution to the civil war was to destroy the source of the SPLA/M's power. The source of the SPLA/M's support was known to the government: the Christians in the south. So, in 1987, the government of Sudan ordered the army to destroy villages in south Sudan. This destruction was aimed to destroy the power of the SPLA/M and to introduce sharia laws and Islamic culture in south Sudan. In 1987, the government destroyed almost all the villages in south Sudan without the intervention of neighboring countries' governments or the international community. So, with the aim of killing specific groups of people in a particular area, was this civil war, genocide, and a holocaust?

The Destruction of Villages in South Sudan

I was born in a small village called Maborkoch near Rumbek town in 1977 in southern Sudan. Life was beautiful and good. However, in 1987 when I was 10 years old, the Islamic government of northern Sudan destroyed my village. The destruction happened around 3 p.m. the time children played outside far way from parents. I was one of the children who were grazing cows and playing as we usually did. Unfortunately, we heard gunshots. When we looked around, we saw helicopter gunships bombing the villages. A few minutes later, those who were fortunate enough to escape the destruction arrived in the bush. Because of gunfire and the bombing, the cows ran back to the villages. The merciless soldiers on the ground did strictly what they were told by the government; they killed people and cows and burned down the entire villages. Those of us who were fortunate enough to live remained in the bush. At around 9 p.m. we went to the villages. There was nothing but dead people and animals, some on fire. That was the end of my beautiful childhood, and I felt that there was no need to live anymore. However, in the same night, something moved me. That something was not fear because I gave up on life and wanted to die, but something in me told me to get up and walk. I got up and walked, not knowing where I was going. So, I walked to the east because the soldiers who destroyed our villages came from the west and north.

From Sudan to Ethiopia

I walked from Rumbek, in southern Sudan, to Ethiopia. I walked for a month. As a group, we walked mostly during the nights to avoid government soldiers, and I ended up in Ethiopia, a neighboring country. I stayed in Ethiopia for four years where another civil war followed. In 1991, I left Ethiopia and moved between the borders until I ended up in Kenya in 1992. We lived in Kenya for nine years and in 2001, I came to the United States.

The Lost Boys who were resettled in the United States wanted to obtain an education, and I have done this but with great effort and sacrifice. Because the airlifts were occurring in 2001, I left before finishing secondary school, so I had to take GED courses. I also had to work to support myself, as refugee status requires that the refugee be self-supporting within three months. Rather than take a couple of years of courses to finish high school, I found a self-paced program and obtained my GED, and then enrolled in Georgia Perimeter College and Clayton State University, where I graduated with a bachelor's degree in management.

I hope to become a teacher so I can take these skills back to South Sudan. I want to lead the effort to bring education to this area of the world that is just beginning to establish the things it needs to be strong. Unfortunately, applying for jobs in Georgia has been disappointing, as I have received no offers. I've recently married a Dinka wife in south Sudan, and will begin again to look for a position in the United States that will enable me to teach. Of the resources needed for a new South Sudan, schools are the most critical. With Majok focusing on wells for our villages, I hope to build schools and programs to help young South Sudanese boys and girls to learn so that they may guide the new country.

—⟁—

When I was first in Pinyudo and we had been organized into groups, I saw him at one of the volleyball competitions between the groups. He was in Group 12 and I was in Group 9. The first thing I noticed was that he spoke Agar Dinka like people in my village, in Rumbek area. When I heard him, I knew he was from my area. Then the next thing I noticed— as a young boy of seven, missing home after many months on the dusty paths across east Africa—he was older, 10 years old, and he wore the traditional scars across his forehead, meaning he was initiated into manhood in the same fashion of the Agar Dinka.

So he was older, and he was from my area, and this was very important. I felt like someone from home was in that group, and the group was located near mine, so we could visit easily. He and I played basketball, volleyball and soccer together. We met at the community dance events at Pinyudo, and we knew the same dances as we were both from Rumbek area of the Lakes region. His is one friendship that has continued to our new home in Clarkston, Georgia, so this is a strong connection from the refugee camp days.

The building of support among the Lost Boys began in the camps, but it continues in the present through many organizations here in the United States that are devoted to assisting Lost Boys and Southern Sudan.

Our Dinka culture, like that of many tribes in southern Sudan, is built around our cattle, and there are many connections between this and every aspect of daily life. An important part of every Dinka's life is the marriage that he makes. It is a matter of growing up knowing that you will marry, you will have many children, and you will be supported by and provide support to a large extended family of aunts and uncles, grandparents, nieces, nephews, cousins, and many others. The marriage will benefit everyone because there will be more children to carry on the tribe. So a large emphasis is on that marriage, and on the bride-price that will be paid in a traditionally orchestrated exchange between the family of the groom and the family of the bride.

The groom's side will negotiate with the family of the bride to determine the number of cattle that will be provided by the groom to the bride's family. There will be gifts from the bride's family as well, but the larger gift will be from the groom, meaning the groom's uncles and cousins and parents and other relatives of the groom as well. Lengthy negotiations ensue—often in a public gathering where other village members can watch—and offers are made back and forth. A beautiful, young, healthy bride with a large or valuable dowry will command a larger number of cattle than one who has less attractive features, physically and resource-wise. The number of cattle is an issue, but also the age and the quality, especially the coloring, of the cattle. Remember that frequently Dinka names, including mine, are derived from the color of cattle—this is like U.S. families giving new babies names of fancy cars, or celebrities, or favorite politicians; it's very important to the culture.

I'm trying to convey the emphasis that is placed on a woman's value in Dinka culture. Her value, her beauty, and her qualities as a woman mean greater monetary and status value in a Dinka marriage. A good marriage is a blessing to the family, as their wealth will increase with a skillful negotiation and securing of such a union.

So it was a bad thing for us to learn, in Kakuma Refugee Camp, that one of the UN-employed teachers was encouraging young girls in her classes to use their bodies to earn money. She was a Kenyan lady who was supposed to be teaching children, boys and girls, but she changed her teaching to mislead the girls. She taught girls how to get money from the market, and she told them that the parts of their bodies were gold, so why not use it to get clothes, shoes, food, lotions and other things. This woman was employed by UNHCR to be a teacher. Yet she was doing the opposite. This was a very negative thing in the refugee girls' lives, to be trained in that way; the teacher took advantage of the fact that there was no way to make income in the camp; the only currency was exchanging the ration of food. So if a young girl wanted lotions, or more food, or clothes, the teacher was showing her an immoral way.

These are some of the issues that refugees faced in the camp. Possibly it was unknown officially to UNHCR while it went on, but it destroyed some young girls' lives. In my culture, such a girl is spoiled for marriage. It was a very bad thing that this teacher did. A lot of people complained about her and she left. Our people don't tolerate that kind of thing because our girls are really the income to the family. Anybody that messes with the girls—the family would not be happy about it. Other cultures may do it, but in Dinka culture it is not good.

Our respect for women is not just because of this custom. Women hold authority in our communities and in our families. It is the sayings of our grandmothers and mothers and aunts that we remembered in times we were separated from family. The women must support the decisions of the men, or they will not happen. Women work extremely hard in our culture, and their lives are often filled with many occasions for sorrow, especially when giving birth. All their days are filled: with working with their men in the field in the morning, then coming in to make food for their children, walking sometimes miles to get water and firewood, grinding grain, then tending the children all day and making meals for the family, providing for clothing and family needs of all kinds. It does not end as an elderly person, for they help their daughters with their families, too.

At Kakuma, another thing we complained about, but it did not change over the nine years I was there, was that women and girls were allowed to go to the UN staff compound at any time. The compound is the group of buildings and tents that housed UNHCR staff as well as refugee aid workers from various humanitarian groups. If you were a man or a boy, you could not go. The exception to this was that a man with a title, such as the chairman of the camp, who would carry identification as chairman, would be allowed into the compound. Or a man or boy who was provided a specific written pass could go. But women and girls did not have to provide any papers. They went all the time.

This made our men very suspicious. A man would say, "Why can my wife go in, and I can't?" There was a great deal of questioning about this, and it often caused a lot of friction in the families, where the husband and wife would separate. Why should an agency devoted to the welfare of refugees inflict such pain on the people it is to help? We never understood why the males could not go beyond the gate to the fenced compound, but women and girls were free to go anytime. More of the world now knows of how sexual enslavement was going on in Darfur and other places where different groups in northern Sudan warred on the people there. But it seems incredible UNHCR or other people would be taking sexual advantage of refugees in their charge.

Another food shortage hit us in 1997, and the distributed food was reduced. Instead of one cup of grain, which was expected, incredibly, to feed us for two weeks, it now became one-half cup. There were some days we did not eat, but saved our ration for the next day. And then there would be another day during those two weeks when we would again go without eating. That was a great hardship. We were playing sports, going to school, and having to deal with the hunger that followed us every day. The ration returned to the full cup eventually.

We slept in shelters that had been constructed by the local Kenyans who were employed in many, many functions throughout the camp. We were three or four to a shelter, and we kept our rations there, cooked there. During the dry season from January to March, the winds blew sand from the desert into our shelters. Often we would wake up covered in sand.

As the years lengthened and more refugees were added, my group changed to Group 17. I attended school with my group, so there were 17 primary schools. I went on into high school. A high school was built in 1997—a large open building with a sheet metal roof, not like our primary school classroom with the palm-leaf cover. We were progressing through our forms, learning the materials for high school proficiency. We were doing all this in English, a big difference from our Dinka, Nuer, and

Murle languages, and different, too, from the Arabic we would have learned in southern Sudan.

The question continually hanging over our heads was what would we do after we finished school? We were getting into our mid- and late teens now. We knew it was not likely we could go to university in Kenya.

In about 1999, UNHCR started meeting with group leaders. They came up with solutions for our future, at least some of us, that involved relocating us overseas. The group leaders and UNHCR then came to meet in the groups with us. It was there that we began to hear the words "resettlement" and "resettlement in the United States." UNHCR staff led discussions focusing us on thinking of our future. They outlined the limited opportunities where we were.

"Where are you going after high school?" the officials asked. We knew that we didn't want to live in the town of Kakuma, where there was no water and no food. They said if we resettled, we could work, go to school, get some vocational training, and start our lives. They had a plan for underage boys and girls to go to the United States as foster children. They said older boys, now becoming or already considered adults, could go in groups and live together to learn about life there with people we knew.

The process of selecting boys to go to the United States started with a list from some old books. When we had first come to the camp at Pinyudo in Ethiopia after our long journeys to find safety there, an organization called Radda Barnen (Swedish for Save the Children) took our pictures. This group was doing a lot of things for us in Pinyudo. They took our pictures, then. About the time of the resettlement talks, one of the same people who had done that project came to see us in Kakuma. He knew us and he met us at Pinyudo. The others that died, he didn't have them on this list, and they said that they didn't make it. So when this person came in from the UN and said they wanted to resettle the minors, they went for the old books that the names were in. These were records from this project that started back in 1989 in Pinyudo. Those records are all we have of our past. They recorded our names, took our pictures, recorded our tribes and sub-tribes, and wrote down what we said in response to the question, "Why are you here? What happened in your village?" So this book has much detail of what we said to the Save the Children people when we were new at the camp in Pinyudo. There are thousands of pictures and papers that say what happened to us. So the UN could identify who arrived first at Pinyudo and who was now at Kakuma.

That is the list that the UN took in deciding who to resettle first. My name was in there. So they went to each group and they called the names. When they went to the groups, sometimes the group has changed, but still they knew you were in a certain group at Pinyudo. That's how they determined who would go.

What happened in Ethiopia is that they would see your physical exam results, and they would give you the year you were born. You may be 18 or seven or 17. They would go by your height. So I was determined to be seven years old. The data base of all these documents is available for all Lost Boys to see on a website devoted to our reunion. It is amazing to see these pictures. Even though my picture is not there (many pictures were lost or perhaps did not turn out good, so are not included), I am grateful to have my home village, my family, and my Agar Dinka tribe listed. I can look and see how many boys in that camp had my first name— there are many! And it is there for all to read: the animal attacks, soldier attacks, thirst, disease, and starvation that the Lost Boys endured on the way.

There were many things to think about in resettling to a new country. The main worry was leaving Sudan and not knowing when we would return. We talked about this among ourselves a lot. But the choice of going or staying was not totally ours. There would be a selection process. The United States would send representatives to talk to us, to see whether we should be among those to be resettled. There would be medical exams to make sure we were healthy enough to go. And there would be training to prepare us for the new country. Most of us had only ridden in minibuses, never a car. We'd not talked on a telephone, much less a cell phone, and had yet to see a television. Our water came mainly from rivers, in our experience, except for the large tanks that held water pumped from many more feet down below us. The idea of cities where miles of pipes carried water across miles and miles of land was beyond anything we had dreamed of.

Many of us wanted to go to the United States. We were anxious to continue our studies. Now that we had been educated in the camp schools, we were ready for more. And we wanted to begin our lives, to learn professions that we could then come back to Sudan and use to build the homes and canals and water systems and electrical grids that the southern part of the country needed.

I had a dream that started back in Poktub, when we saw all the cranes and the equipment building the Jonglei Canal. There were buildings and roads and large tractors and structures like I had never seen. It opened my eyes, those three months we spent making and selling our goods to the people there, to the fact that we had none of that kind of development anywhere in my village or anywhere near Rumbek. The project was now stalled, but even so, there were water systems and buildings and roads and some electricity—all things we did not have in my village.

All those things we needed, but our politicians that we sent from southern Sudan to Khartoum to represent us never brought the things we needed, like water systems, clinics, housing, and electricity, and the politicians just stayed in Khartoum. Meanwhile, the oil that was only on southern Sudan's land was pumped to northern Sudan and the money for that went to and stayed in Khartoum. No wonder my village and all the others in southern Sudan did not have the things they needed!

Reflecting on what I'd seen at Poktub, I decided I wanted to go to college to learn how to be a geologist, so I could find more oil in Sudan. Only this would be oil to benefit my area.

Some discussions began in 1999, but it was late in November 2000 before the possibility of resettlement became real. And then it happened very quickly. Through that process I just mentioned, boys were first selected after they had been identified in the old books from Pinyudo. We came out of our groups. Then we were interviewed by U.S. immigration staff. Mobile clinics were set up along with classrooms to give instruction for those being resettled. Our names came up on a board, and we went through physical exams and an orientation course.

The course helped us understand about cold weather or other conditions and how to prepare for it, we were educated on the money system that was the basis of the economy in the United States, we were told how to prepare for going to school in the new city and many more new things to anticipate in our new homes. We were told about our sponsors and how important they would be and about other agencies that would help us in the transition. We would live together in groups in our first homes, so we would have each other.

Then a plane swept in from Nairobi, landing on a field near where we were. This was the airfield for the town of Kakuma, but it was next to our camp. And then the first Lost Boys—those who were younger than 18 and who would become part of foster families in the United States—boarded the plane and took off for Nairobi and eventually for destinations in the United States. There were two flights a day with a total of about 95 Lost Boys. A total of 400 underage boys and girls left, and they were resettled with families, with a large majority going to Phoenix, Arizona. Another 40 went to Mississippi. Others of the underage boys and girls went to Boston, Connecticut, Pennsylvania and Michigan.

The plane arrived in the morning, and it took a load of 46 or 47. The plane flew to Nairobi, Kenya, and let the passengers out. The plane that had delivered them to Nairobi turned around and came for another load that left at 2 p.m. From Nairobi, the refugees then boarded a flight to Amsterdam. From there they flew to New York and then to their destination cities.

So over several days this unheard of spectacle unfolded—many young men and women walking up a ramp into a plane, their many friends watching from behind a fence as they took off into the sky like a bird or a vulture, disappearing into the sky.

In early 2001, Lost Boys now 18 and over were identified and went through the same process. I was in the first group of the 18-year-old Lost Boys to leave Kakuma. We had interviews with Immigration, and then very quickly we had our physicals and went through a shortened orientation—all this happened in four days. That's when I found out I would be one of six going to Atlanta, Georgia. My three roommates and I would be sponsored by Lutheran Ministries of Georgia, which is now known as Lutheran Services of Georgia (LSG).

The roommates I would have were Tingke Poundak Reec, who was Agar Dinka from the same area I was; Mapuor Mabor Pur, a Cic Dinka from my area also; and Makuol Akuei, a Tuic Dinka from Jonglei province (this is the province where the canal was being built where my original group stayed for three months on the way to Ethiopia). Tingke was actually not in our travel group, but arrived one day after we arrived in Georgia.

All I knew of the United States was the airports we would visit during this trip—New York City and D.C. I knew nothing of Georgia. The only states that I was familiar with at all were North and South Dakota, as that is where some in our camp were resettled during the mid– and late 1990s.

On February 12, we were on the morning plane. On the plane were 43 who would go to several locations: Atlanta, Virginia, Vermont, Salt Lake City, and California. In fact, my cousin Kolnyin Nak Goljok—he is my mother's elder sister's son—was in Kakuma Camp and was on our plane; he traveled with us as far as New York. His final destination was San Jose, California, where he still lives, working for Home Depot.

At each juncture of our trip, there was a representative of the IOM, the International Organization for Migration, to make sure that we got to the next point and that our papers were processed. This happened at each transfer point except for the final connection.

We were whisked off to Nairobi where we waited in the airport for many hours. When we came into Nairobi and saw below us the sprawling city and the tall buildings, I experienced again that anger at our politicians for not working for us in southern Sudan to get the buildings and the businesses and the roads and communications that we saw there in Nairobi. In this country right next to southern Sudan, there was incredible development. In Rumbek, our only large town, there were only one-story buildings. Where were our streets and electricity and all those things that Kenya had?

Then we got on a huge plane that took us to Amsterdam. We stayed overnight in a hotel, and then we flew the next day to JFK airport in New York City. When we were going through customs at JFK, one of our group asked to use the restroom. It was a highly secure restroom, with locks on the outside door, and he was told not to close the door completely. The door closed anyway, and it locked him in, and there was no one in the area at the time with a key. We waited and finally someone with a key came and got him out. We were really worried that he'd never get out.

We spent the night in a big hotel in New York. Another problem happened when we were being collected at the hotel the next morning to return to the airport. We all had different flights because we were going to several U.S. cities. The person who came up and got us called them on the phone, but they didn't pick up. We waited for like two hours, and then they had to make a check on every room that had a Lost Boy. So that was like 43 boys, two people to a room. So we finally got there to the airport.

We flew to Washington Dulles, and here we were on our own. We found our gate, and since there were no papers to process, we did not need assistance. We stayed there for three hours. Then we took off and arrived in Atlanta on February 14 in the evening, about 5 or 6 o'clock. We were met by a caseworker from Lutheran Services of Georgia, a Somalian guy named Mustafa Noor, and he brought us to an apartment at Kensington Manor in Stone Mountain, Georgia. He moved us in with things like dining area furniture and mattresses on the floor and a telephone.

It was really cold, and there was no heat. Our unit was on the first level, way down below, with two floors above us. There was a creek that was going by, so it seemed even colder. Also, the one toilet in the apartment did not work. We had electricity. So there was a stove, and we tried to heat the apartment with the heat from the stove. This was at night when we arrived, so in the morning we tried to find the management office. We went there, and we asked for repairs, and they said they would take care of it, but they didn't. We asked for blankets, and we didn't get that. We were freezing, as it was February in Atlanta, and we were not happy.

We managed day to day, but it was not good. We were cold all the time. We had a phone and we made calls. Lutheran Services of Georgia was our sponsor, so we called them when we needed things. Our names were not on the lease; it may have been our sponsor's.

Our task was to find jobs right away. There was some financial assistance to us for three months, and then we were to be on our own, paying our own rent and utilities. So getting a job was what we tried to do right away. Lutheran Services had caseworkers who helped us find jobs; they also had caseworkers who could help us apply for food stamps. We applied for everything.

One day at our apartment, a lady came to see us who was a volunteer. Her name was Cyndie Heiskell, and she saw how poorly we were living. She also told us that she had heard of the Lost Boys a long time before. In fact, she had dreams about us before much was known in the United States about our civil war. She said she'd been trying to find out about us ever since the dreams. Finally, through a chance meeting at her church with someone who'd been in Sudan, she was able to connect with us.

Cyndie even knew the name of the person from the United States who had died in a plane crash trying to come see us at Pinyudo. It was U.S. Congressman Mickey Leland of Texas, who had made several trips to Ethiopia and Sudan in an attempt to see if he could get the United States to do something to help the refugees. It was a tragedy that he had died. How close we had come to getting aid earlier—maybe even U.S. help in stopping the war! It was interesting to me that Cyndie knew so much about our situation. It was gratifying to hear that some in the United States had tried to help us, even long ago.

Cyndie's father was a former Coca-Cola executive who had started the first canning plant for Cokes. Her parents subsequently founded a private school in Atlanta, and she was the director of the school, the

Heiskell School. She was a very powerful person. She talked to somebody in D.C., and that's when they moved all our things to Le Carre apartments. The director of Lutheran Services of Georgia came and moved us to Le Carre, a much better apartment.

In the meantime—and this was all within our first month in Georgia—we got jobs, all at the DeKalb Farmers Market, so we did not need those food stamps after all. The DeKalb Farmers Market was a bus ride away and could be walked as well if need be. We were in the produce area: Table One, Table Two and Table Three. We were in different shifts. Tingke was in the first shift. I was in second shift. Makuol and Mapour were in the third shift, where they started at three and got off at nine.

We set about making a life in Georgia. We worked and shopped and found our way around Atlanta, on a limited basis, for we depended on MARTA (Metropolitan Atlanta Rapid Transit Authority) and rides from others. LSG and other volunteer agencies supplied our apartments with furniture, a TV, and basic needs. We learned how to take a MARTA bus. We were given orientations through LSG and took English as a Second Language classes. About that time, too, we tried to find a Catholic church nearby, and we called Corpus Christi Catholic Church in Stone Mountain. We were referred to Gini Eagen at the church, and she tried to help us find our way by using local buses. We attempted the trip, which involved some bus transfers, but it didn't work out. So we called her again. This time, she offered to come ride with us so we would not get lost.

The lady who showed up to help us was tall and thin and blond, and she was surprised to find so many Sudanese who were Catholic. There were probably 10 of us that day, as in talking to people in our classes or in our apartments, we found there were quite a few local Sudanese. Well, we got on the buses and we transferred, but in the end, we had to walk quite a way, too. So here was blonde Gini leading all of us very dark, sometimes very tall Sudanese, down Memorial Drive and down the next streets to get to church. But we got to hear Mass for the first time in our new country, and it was very welcoming.

After Gini talked to us for a while she learned that there were a number of aid agencies providing a variety of services and food, job advice, English lessons and other needs. She felt the best thing the church could do to help us was to provide a Mass in our community so that we did not have to go through the arduous double bus transfer and walking method to hear Mass. So for several years, from that time on, Father Kenny, pastor at Corpus Christi, Gini, and Father Jose Kochuparampil, made sure that each Sunday afternoon at 2 p.m. the Sudanese community in Clarkston heard Mass at Clarkston Community Center. Father Jose was our usual celebrant, and the Corpus Christi parish social welfare fund paid the cost of rental for the building.

Many Sudanese families were able to join us, and we had a community of 70 or 80 on a regular basis. Being dependent on public transportation or our feet, it was a great blessing to be able to walk to our weekly Mass and to worship together as we had in Kakuma Refugee Camp.

The church's funds also paid for special needs in the Sudanese community over the next several years. Gini became our sounding board when we had difficulties or needed help making an important decision. Because she was an older woman and because she did so much for us, it was natural for us to start calling her "Mama Gini." She reminded us so much of our mothers and grandmothers in the villages we came from. And Mama Gini made a special contribution of her own energies which I'll write about later on.

On the evening of September 11, 2001, we were at our apartment, except for Makuol. We heard the news about the attacks on the World Trade Towers during the day, and we watched television news about the event. We were surprised we had come so far to get away from such attacks, and now they were happening here in the United States. Makuol was coming home from the market after his shift ended at 9. A friend had given him a ride to Clarkston, and he got out of the car and turned onto our street, a few blocks from our apartment. When he got near our apartment, he was jumped by six toughs.

"You from Africa?" they yelled at him as they started beating him. "You bombed the towers?" Makuol ran away, up to our apartment, and was breathing really heavily when he came in and told us what had happened. But he'd gotten away. One thing Lost Boys can do is run—fast.

That night someone broke the glass in the patio door of our balcony. The next night six cars all had glass broken. We called our LSG contacts, and some of the people we knew at a local foundation that was being created, the Lost Boys Foundation. Before we knew it, we were being interviewed by CNN and the local television news stations and there were stories about us everywhere—Lost Boys beat up because people thought we were Islamic terrorists! And we were fleeing the war caused by Islamists ourselves!

Even the FBI came in. Cyndie called them, and an agent came with her. Within one week they caught the guys, but Makuol declined to identify them. Three guys came three times trying to get him to identify the suspects, but he wouldn't.

We had had people like Cyndie and Lutheran Services and Corpus Christi and others helping us, but now there were even more volunteers. One lady came to visit at our apartment when she heard about the attack. Her name was Ann Mahoney, and her husband, Fred Rossini, and she provided a great deal of assistance to our boys. Ann tutored us in our English, and her husband gave us the gift of mobility. He taught each of us how to drive! That was very exciting, because we knew from our experiences that having a car was very important in Atlanta. For some of us, it took a while to pass the test—we could get much of what was required, but some of it did not come so easily. But eventually we all passed and got our drivers' licenses.

—◊—

FROM TEETH TO DRIVING,
VOLUNTEERS HELP THE NEW RESIDENTS

On September 11, 2001, Ann Mahoney was a volunteer ESOL tutor interested in helping people who were truly marginalized improve their English. She lived in the Little 5 Points neighborhood of Atlanta, and after the fall of the Twin Towers, she saw a report in the Atlanta Journal-Constitution about Makuol Akuei being attacked near his apartment in Clarkston after the terrorists' attack.

"It seemed in the article he'd been targeted as a non–American," she said, "and he looked vulnerable to some other people, too. He was caught in that violent response by some desperate people following 9/11 of 'getting even.'"

Ann met Makuol and his roommates at that time, including Majok Marier. Makuol later went to live with Waal and Mading, "who were from his clan," she said.

Ann worked with Makuol on his English skills. Fred Rossini, her late husband, a Georgia Tech physics professor and former provost of George Mason University, "taught several of the guys to drive. They did the practice things so they could go take the test"—no easy task for men who'd never even ridden a bicycle.

Makuol's front tooth was abscessed and Ann took him to their dentist, whose heart was touched by his situation and discounted her services.

After Makuol got training as a nursing assistant (CNA), the couple tried to help him get a job in a nursing home in the Atlanta area.

"That was difficult," she said. "Sometimes he would know they'd hired other people.... He recognized the prejudice here." Eventually, he moved to Iowa where he could get financial aid for college classes, and was successful in working in a nursing home there. Ann said she felt this was due to his love and respect for old people, a key element of Dinka culture.

Ann said there were problems in the jobs the boys held early in their lives in Georgia. At the farmers' market where they worked, there was a dispute with an Ethiopian in the area where one of the boys worked.

"There became a bad scene with bad feelings, and they all walked out in solidarity," she recalled. From there, some went to work at a meat-packaging plant south of Atlanta.

"They'd be picked up early to go to the plant. They'd have to stay until the very last person was allowed to leave at night—often very late at night."

After Majok finished training as a plumber's helper, Ann asked her plumber about openings in his business, and as he did not offer benefits, he referred Majok to his current employer, M. Cary and Daughters, where he could earn benefits, which they all thought important.

"That's what people who transplant themselves from a different culture come and arrive without," Ann said. "The scariest thing is that there's nobody to fall back on if you're in a pinch." She became that backstop for Makuol, paying for his travel to Sudan and back a couple of times as, after the war ended, he married a Dinka wife and had a son. Tragically, this baby died of malaria. Makuol is currently studying at the University of Northern Iowa and is close to completing his bachelor's degree. He and his wife had another son earlier this year.

One of the things Ann noticed when she went to the boys' first apartment was that they laid down textiles—all colors, not just bright colors—on the floor.

"It made me wonder if that's what you do when you have a dirt floor," she said, referring to their homes in South Sudan. "It did create a feeling of coziness.

"They cooked these big pots of soup or stew for everyone." Ann was impressed "that they knew how to take care of each other. I know there were four people in the original apartment. Eventually when Simon [Makuol] was staying with Mading and John, it impressed me that it was somewhat flexible who would be staying there. I kinda had the sense that they didn't

have this wall around 'these are who live here.' Different people would be there at different times."

Ann admired the Lost Boys' basic skills and mindset of survival that caused them to overcome extreme hardships in their trek across East Africa. Now she sees the "element of being really vulnerable and not having most of our American-style defense mechanisms—all those things that worked so well for them in the beginning part of their life," and wonders, "how are they working now in our culture?"

Those good qualities—the reliance on elders for guidance, perseverance that helped them survive, their lack of defense mechanisms—"those are what people in this country overlook when they speak negatively about immigration," she said. "We have to learn to notice these values, for goodness' sake. It seems like our [American] culture is getting impoverished in a lot of human ways, and I think an infusion of people who are so close to what's really basic to the heart and survival" is good for the United States.

"I feel enriched by knowing these guys," Ann said.

—⁂—

About a year after we'd arrived, we four left our jobs at the DeKalb Farmers Market. Mama Gini was a big help when I was looking for work and planning to go to school. She helped me find a job fair for part-time jobs, and I worked a little while for Regal Cinemas. Mapour found another job with Walmart. Tingke went with Makuol to work at a meat-packaging company in Newnan. I later got a job with Grand Hyatt working in banquet services.

One of the volunteers who was working with us found out about the Job Corps program. Makuol and I went for the training that they offered. It was in Washington, D.C.; I attended from May 2002 until the end of 2003, and I was able to complete high school and to get diplomas in plumbing and in data entry. Makuol was able to complete high school and to get a diploma as a nursing assistant. One of the good things about Job Corps was that we could get some training, and then we could stay at the Job Corps Center and eat our meals there and work during the day while stopping out of the Job Corps programs for a while. That way we could work and use the skills we were learning and not lose our place at the school. Then we could finish high school and graduate.

Once we returned to Atlanta, Ann Mahoney knew we were looking for jobs, and she offered to help. It was through Ann that I met my current employer, M. Cary and Daughters Plumbing Company, where I'm a plumber. Makuol tried to get a job in a clinic or hospital, but he was unsuccessful. So he left for Iowa, and he is working in nursing there even today. One of the things that I am grateful for in my employer is, first, I am able to work in the field for which I was educated, and second, my employer allows me to travel overseas for an extended visit when I am able to save money to travel so that I can be with my family. As long as I am back on the job when I say I will return, they allow this leave of absence.

When I was a young boy, I was lucky to survive the bombing and gunfire at my village, the long walk to Ethiopia, then back to Sudan, and then to Kenya, even though thirst and starvation and wild animals and enemies with spears or guns and bombs threatened us. As young men, we had difficulties in our transition in Georgia, but we survived this also with the many volunteers and organizations who helped us. There were so many who helped whose names I do not recall, and many whose names I never knew. With their many actions and gifts of generosity and God's aid, we are here today. But we think constantly about our brothers and our families back home and what to do to help them.

Eight

America's Struggle Ends Sudanese Airlifts

After my companions and I lifted off from Kakuma, many others followed. In time, 4,000 Lost Boys, including the 400 underage boys and girls who left in 2000, were flown out of the camp. Lost Boys went to cities all over the United States as various groups sponsored their resettlement in their towns. While many agencies we knew were providing us assistance in Clarkston, similar aid was going to the boys in those other cities.

A network among all the boys was begun through their sponsoring organizations. As our sponsor was the Lutheran Services of Georgia, and they had associated ministries in other states, they were able to tell us where other Lost Boys were and how to contact them. We had telephones in our apartments, and as soon as we knew where some of our friends had resettled and we got their phone numbers, we called them. Today, we still keep in touch, either by phone or the Internet. Or sometimes we hear through visits of others to those other cities. In a few cases, we have visited other large groups in other cities. For instance, we traveled to Syracuse and to Nashville. We stay in close touch with groups in Greensboro, North Carolina, and other cities not too far away.

The War on Terror had great implications for us. This was the United States going against the types of enemies we had suffered from for decades. There was an instant recognition that this was our fight as well.

On the other hand, because of the nature of the attack and the fact that it had come by terrorists using commercial airlines, the airlifting of

Majok and friend decorate apartment for Christmas 2009, Atlanta.

Lost Boys stopped. Perhaps another flight or two came in, but that was it. It was as though the terror brought to the U.S. shores also brought a heightened fear of those from the continents where Osama Bin Laden and Al Qaida on the Arabian Peninsula had been active. Again, Sudan was not Somalia. But it was close enough to be caught in the group of nations from which the United States now wanted to protect itself. It definitely shifted the focus of U.S. efforts to resettle more Sudanese. It was a dramatic change, to say the least.

Now we knew that just as the United States went after Osama, there was little hope for those many other boys in camps like Kakuma. The closing of the door to them left us feeling that we needed to do whatever we could to help. And it pushed us to become the best that we could so that we could make the refugee camps no longer necessary in East Africa.

While there were great needs overseas, we found that our minor celebrity in the Atlanta community helped to create bridges and more understanding of our country and its plight. People in the Atlanta community helped us with finances and came forth when there were difficulties among our members. Gabriel Buol, one of our boys, was diagnosed with liver cancer. He died in 2005 in a Hospice Atlanta facility, after receiving many, many visits from us, his volunteer "mother," Janis Sundquist, and loving care from his Nigerian nurse, Matthew Ojo. It was difficult to see Gabriel die after he had survived so much in Sudan. The news media wrote stories about him that went around the country, and his death greatly saddened all of us. Corpus Christi helped us raise the money that is necessary for a funeral in the United States—even a very simple burial. Our profile also helped the other Sudanese in the Atlanta community. When a mother lost a daughter to a stabbing death in Michigan, the body needed to be returned to Atlanta and a funeral provided. A three-year-old Sudanese boy, here only a week, was struck and killed by a car. The Lost Boys, who knew English and who now were becoming skilled in working with organizational structures, were able to access aid and translation help for the Sudanese newcomers in their dealings with local authorities.

With the assistance of Mama Gini at Corpus Christi Catholic Church in Stone Mountain, we began meeting to find ways of helping our communities back home. Lost Boys from other cities who were from Dinka tribes gathered several times in Stone Mountain. We formed an organization called Rumbek Youth Vision, as most of us were from villages in or near Rumbek, and most of these are from the Agar Dinka tribe. The association was incorporated with the assistance of a lawyer in Nashville, Tennessee. We used the foundation as a means of assuring donors that we were not taking the contributions for ourselves, but to directly benefit our home community.

In Sudan, each of us lived in villages without water wells. All of us could have easily said that was the most pressing need. The cost of drilling a single well, because water is about as deep as an 18-story building is tall, is about $50,000 to $100,000. We also need medical clinics in our areas. All of those expenses are far beyond what we can provide. But we raised funds anyway, knowing that whatever we gathered would be more than what was available to young people in southern Sudan at the present. The enthusiasm of the boys to help those back home was very high.

During this time, about 2004, we were befriended by another of our American "mothers," Judy Maves. Judy and her husband, Bill Snodgrass, were very helpful to us over many years, and she helped the boys with immigration papers for themselves and the wives, when the marriages occurred. Judy helped me buy a car, my used Toyota that has been so nec-

John Manyok Anyieth, with parents Bill Snodgrass and Judy Maves at May 2012 graduation from Georgia Perimeter College.

essary for work. She and others also were a key part of another important history-making event for the Lost Boys, an incident I'll relate here soon.

Judy became so involved with us that she and Bill adopted John Manyok Anyieth, one of the boys she met when she volunteered to mentor Lost Boys. Since then, after many years of assisting us, she and Bill have retired to Kenya, near Mombasa, hoping to be closer to boys returning to South Sudan. John has begun work on his bachelor's degree at Clayton State University after finishing his associate's degree at Georgia Perimeter College.

—⟶⟵—

JUDY MAVES AND THE MANY WAYS OF MOTHERING

Judy Maves was an Atlanta-based sales representative and traveled by air a great deal when 9/11 occurred. Like many Americans whose work lives were affected, she flew less and made some career changes afterwards. In

2004, she said, "I read a little article in the Dunwoody Crier *looking for mentors for the Lost Boys."*

She was given two names to call, and one was John Manyok Anyieth, a now 30-year-old man but at the time a young refugee with a need for assistance negotiating the complex American systems. During Sudanese Army attacks in 1987, he had fled his home area of Bor in southern Sudan, lived in refugee camps for many years, and survived many traumatic events. In 1991, Bor in South Sudan was the site of a two-week long massacre in a feud between two groups fighting for control in the rebel SPLA.[1]

"John ended up living with us, and we adopted him," Judy said. She met Majok and many of the young men in their circle. She and her husband provided financial assistance for many needs of the other boys as well.

"I spent my own money and time helping the guys out," Judy said. "Day or night. Clothes, doctors, car purchases. I used to joke that I have become everything from a lawyer to a mechanic."

John recently completed his associate's degree at Georgia Perimeter College and is now studying for a bachelor's degree in business at Clayton State University in Morrow.

Judy and Bill have retired to an area near the Indian Ocean outside of Mombasa, Kenya. But it's probably more a location from which to do more for South Sudan.

"After working with the Lost Boys, I grew to love South Sudan and Africa and wanted to live there," she said. "I knew we'd need to make the transition before we got too old to make that change because living in Africa is a very different experience. I hoped to be near South Sudan when the boys came back." Yet she finds herself coming back to Atlanta frequently due to the boys continuing to live here rather than in their original home. And she needs to visit her son, John.

"After having John live with us for nine years, leaving him to finish school was the hardest thing I have ever done," she said of her only child.

In 2011, she helped organize the caravan of cars traveling back and forth from Nashville when the men went to vote in the historic independence referendum. Hit with a historic snowstorm on their return to Atlanta, they slid into a car at the highest point of the elevated freeway ramp leading from I-75 South to I-285 and got stuck with many other cars on that ramp.

"Eighteen-wheelers were just barely missing us, we were really frightened," she said. "We pulled the cars out, then John drove the car down to 285 going five miles an hour. Then 12 of us—including Majok—locked arms

and walked very slowly down the ramp to get in the car and the other one we'd freed.

"There are several of the guys that I have helped with immigration papers for themselves and their wives," she said. On the ways she was asked to help: "The list is endless, but rewarding. I helped solve problems with some I never thought I was capable of."

Her many efforts have extended to South Sudan itself. She represents Raising South Sudan from Atlanta, a nonprofit project with support from Mothering Across Continents, a Charlotte-based collaborative that works to bring schools, water and other needs to third-world countries. Patricia Shafer, who also was on the trip to Nashville and hired a professional film crew to accompany the group, is the chief catalyst, or executive director, of Mothering Across Continents. She actively provides technical resources and development assistance for needed facilities in South Sudan.

So far, one school with four classrooms, two offices, latrines and a reha-bilitated well has been built in one location in Unity State, South Sudan, and another is under development. Both of these have Southern U.S.-based Lost Boys, James Lubo Mijak and Ngor Kur Mayol, working with the local villages on the schools and raising funds in the United States.

"I wanted to try to help each one achieve his goals, whether it be in education, to marry, help their people back home or just find a job," Judy said. Her desire to help led to a new home in Africa, becoming a mother, and providing hundreds of acts of assistance to the Lost Boys as they continue their journey both in America and South Sudan.

—w—

Finally, in 2005, a cease-fire was declared in the war with Sudan, a war that had started when the Sudanese government tried to enforce sharia law throughout the country. The Sudanese Army and the Sudanese Liberation Peoples' Army reached an accord, called the Comprehensive Peace Agreement (CPA), that laid out a plan for ending the fighting. In the agreement, it was stated that in five and a half years, in January 2011, there would be a referendum that would allow the people of southern Sudan to decide if they wanted to be an independent country. There was great rejoicing—not only in southern Sudan, but in Clarkston, Syra-cuse, Nashville, Greensboro, California, Vermont, Mississippi, Kansas City, and all the places where Lost Boys and other large Sudanese com-munities lived. Now peace had come, and there would be a new country. We could plan a future that included going home. We would possibly be

Stephen Chol Bayok greets his mother after 20-year separation. His grandmother (right, sitting beside them) looks on.

in the United States for a while yet in order to become educated with skills to lead the new country of South Sudan. But we would be able to go home.

Our families were still in flux, still not back in their villages, probably. We did not know in many cases where our families were. Communication with a family was all by word of mouth, as there are few landline telephones in South Sudan, and there is no postal system. If someone went to Sudan and they returned and told you they had seen someone, a relative, that is how you found out about them. I didn't know where my family was or even who was alive after this long war.

John Garang, the leader of the SPLA and the Sudanese Peoples' Liberation Movement (SPLM), was hailed as a hero. A former Sudanese Army officer who joined a mass SA defection to resist the Khartoum government back in 1983, he was to play a major role in a Unity Government, also called for in the CPA, that would rule in the six years before the referendum. There were to be representatives of the ruling Islamic political party as well as the SPLM running the country. He was first vice president, and also the administrator of South Sudan. Unfortunately, he died with a dozen others when his helicopter crashed three weeks after he took office in July 2005. This set off riots among southern Sudanese in Khartoum and Juba, and the mystery of why the helicopter crashed has never been solved.

Nevertheless, the SPLM and its large army took the lead in working to see that a peaceful process was observed and that the government made good on its parts of the CPA, especially preparing for elections set to occur in early 2011. The Lost Boys who were part of the Rumbek Youth Vision accelerated plans to go back to Sudan, especially after Stephen Chol Bayok, my friend from back in Pinyudo Camp, heard that his mother was alive and efforts were made to make contact with her. After a very long and difficult effort involving his mother traveling to Uganda to stay and to telephone him, the two were reunited over the phone, and he made plans to meet her. Others were able to hear, also, or were planning to go to find their relatives once they arrived in the Rumbek area. Likewise, I submitted my application for a travel document from what was then called the Immigration and Naturalization Service (now Immigration and Customs Enforcement). Unfortunately, these did not come in time, and I was unable to go.

—∞—

MAMA GINI GOES TO SUDAN

Gini Eagen, known to the Lost Boys in Clarkston, Georgia, as Mama Gini, is a pastoral associate at Corpus Christi Catholic Church in Stone Mountain, Georgia. In 2001, she heard about the Lost Boys resettling in nearby Clarkston. She said she initially resisted getting involved.

"Once they entered my life, I knew my life would be forever changed," she said. *"I knew I could never be simply a bystander, but they would enter into my heart and soul,"* she said. *"This has proved to be true."*

Corpus Christi is served by the Claretian Fathers, an order of Roman Catholic priests that has a worldwide presence, but that has for many years operated in Latin America. Most of the priests are bilingual in Spanish, and Corpus Christi has about 80 countries represented among its parishioners. So it was not unusual for the Lost Boys to contact the church.

Gini tried to tell them how to get to the church. After the directions using MARTA resulted in their getting lost on Memorial Drive, Gini drove to their apartments to ride MARTA with them. This proved difficult as well, as the bus let them out and they still had to walk a long way. So, with the help of the pastor, Father Greg Kenny, Gini arranged to have a special Mass celebrated for the boys and for other members of the Sudanese community each Sunday afternoon at Clarkston Community Center.

The pastor, Father Greg Kenny, and then Father Jim Curran followed by Father Jose Kochuparampil, said the Mass every Sunday over several years. Worship was full of song and joy and African drums. Meeting in community was a great help to the boys as well as the other Sudanese community members, most of whom did not have transportation. Gini recognized that a number of agencies and volunteers were assisting the boys, so the church looked for ways of helping that were not already occurring.

"We began meeting here at Corpus Christi with Lost Boys from the Rumbek area that lived in different parts of the United States," Gini related. "This group of young men knew that they could not solve all the problems of southern Sudan, but they felt compelled to do something for those they left behind. It weighed heavily on them to know that they had food and shelter and opportunities for education and work, when those they left behind had none of these things."

Also about this time, the young men began to hear that family members were still alive—family who thought they were long dead. The began to try to reach their relatives, while at the same time making a plan to gather the youth of the Rumbek area, to bring them hope and establish an organization with which they could communicate across the continents that separated them.

Simple communications that most Americans take for granted are difficult in South Sudan. A good example of this is the lengthy process of connecting Stephen Chol Bayok with his mother. A friend in Uganda called Stephen and said he had been in Sudan and had seen Stephen's mother. This was the first news for Stephen that his mother survived the civil war. Stephen's mother had to travel to Uganda, a distance of 300 miles, with almost no roads, in order to use a telephone to call Stephen in Clarkston. Southern Sudan has historically been left out of Sudan's infrastructure development, and the 22-year civil war also knocked out any existing communication links.

Stephen, who at the time had a job in maintenance at Georgia State University, started working two full-time jobs to earn the $400 for his friend to take his mother to Uganda and support her while she was there. Gini found out about the extra jobs; knowing two jobs and little sleep would jeop-

ardize Stephen's health, she raised the money, and several months later, Stephen's mother called him. He recognized her voice, but she could not believe he was her Stephen. She grilled him about family members. When she finally realized this was her son, she fainted. The scene repeated itself many more times over the next years with more Lost Boys.

For a couple of years, the group of Rumbek area Lost Boys met, and they formed the Rumbek Youth Vision Association. As the long war that had cast them on American shores drew to a close, their plans to return took on a new energy. They could go back to Sudan and perhaps find family, and they could inspire the young men in the villages they had left. Their planning finally culminated in a trip scheduled for December 26, 2005. The boys always assumed Mama Gini, as the project manager for the trip, would go with them. Gini was not so sure, but in August 2005, her husband of many years, Dennis Eagen, died suddenly. After this great loss, Gini decided to make the trip. She felt she was destined to accompany the boys on what would be a spiritual journey for sure.

Eight Lost Boys, a Rwandan refugee worker, and Gini—blond, 64, and grandmotherly—flew to Uganda in late December. Clarkston residents Stephen Bayok, James Maliet, Moses Poundak, and James Malual, along with Lost Boys from other states, made the trip. They stayed at a Ugandan mission station of the Missionaries of the Poor. Gini was well acquainted with the missionaries, as she organized and accompanied more than a dozen annual trips where Corpus Christi parishioners assisted the MOP brothers in Jamaica as they ministered to the poor and destitute there.

The missionaries helped them obtain the paperwork needed in order to fly to Sudan. It was a small airline that flew them, and the boys were concerned about that and about making the trip into Sudan.

"On our return trip to Kampala, Uganda we were surprised when the pilots asked us for money to help fuel the plane on a stop before we got to Kampala," Gini said. The pilots did not have the right kind of currency. Their currency was not the right year of issue. The U.S. currency their passengers had was more acceptable to the man dispensing the fuel than that of the pilots. Some banks did not exchange certain years of U.S. dollars—possibly because of counterfeit money being floated there recently, Gini said. "We weren't exactly sure why—all we knew is that some of our money they would take, but not the pilots." When the plane landed in Rumbek, Sudan, Gini was surprised that the town they had spoken of so much was so undeveloped. The plane appeared to land in a field of dust. No tarmac—only a dirt field.

They were all so welcoming, Gini said. *"Later, in a village, we were standing by a fence made of sticks, and they showed me this large cow with these great horns and I was admiring the horns, and then suddenly the cow was on its back and it was at my feet and its throat was slit,"* Gini said. *"Then I was supposed to step over it before meeting the people who'd come to greet us. As the honored guest, I was expected to step over first. That's when I came face to face with a very important ritual in Sudan.*

"They think the ritual comes from Bible stories that the Christian people heard about but could not read for themselves—the Old Testament story of Moses' sacrifice. They believe when you step over the animal, your sins are forgiven. And it's especially important to perform if people are being reunited after a long absence. That way, if the shock of seeing the other people again causes someone to die, that person would be at peace."

Stephen's reunion with his mother was a high point of the trip.

"It took us a while to find Stephen's mother," Gini said. *"I'm not sure how we found her, as there are no roads with which to give direction. We got out of the truck and walked on rough ground through high grasses, and when we got there she wasn't there. It was very disappointing. Then we went another day, and she was there and his grandma was there. The two got to meet and embrace. It was very moving. To have been part of that—it's something."*

Three goats were slaughtered in a later ceremony honoring Stephen. Gini stepped with him over each of the goats, as she was also being honored. His brother had provided one goat, and his uncles the other two. In fact, at each gathering where a Lost Boy found his family, there was a joyful reunion, and at each one the ceremonial slaughter to welcome the visitors.

The Dinka do not have a great deal of meat in their diet—it is primarily from grains, groundnuts and vegetables grown in their gardens. The cattle are their wealth, used for marriages and sometimes to settle debts or fines; the same is true of other livestock. During marriage negotiations, members of extended families will offer some of their cattle in order to secure the marriage. The groom will later be expected to contribute to other family members' marriage dowries just as he has benefited from their gifts.

But then they were on to the next village, as their goal was to invite the youth of all these five villages that make up the Rumbek area to a meeting "under the trees," the expression they use for coming together for support and decision-making. They told the people in the villages that they were lucky to be alive, and they wanted to share their message of hope, and to share dinner under the trees the following Saturday. So the full reunions had to wait until after they had this meeting at the end of the first week.

So they all gathered, and the boys told what had happened to them in their journeys during the war. They said that they were committed to helping them, but that their resources would be very limited. The most they wanted to share was their hope—if they had survived these terrible tragedies in the civil war, then there was hope for them in their villages, in the new Sudan.

Seeing the needs that were remaining in their villages, the Rumbek Youth Vision organization went back to Clarkston and other towns and raised $3,500; with that money, they purchased and distributed satellite-operated cell phones for each of their villages.

"We were there two weeks," Gini said. "In the second week, the boys did spend time with their families. During that first week of travelling to the five areas, there was one place, Maper, where the boys did not want me to travel with them. It was 75 miles away, a rough five-hour ride over cow paths. Apparently there were some tribal fights still going on in that area, and it was considered dangerous.

"That was when I told them that if the reason they didn't want me to go was because I was a white American woman and that would cause a problem for them, I would understand that," Gini said. "But if it was simply because they were concerned for my safety, that wasn't fair because I was part of the group. And so they met—they were always meeting—and they came back and said I could go."

So they came to pick her up in an SUV the next morning at 3 a.m. The SUV was carrying an extra passenger—a guard with a rifle. The local leaders had provided a car and security for the trip. The area they went to was hard to access in dry season, which this was, and cut off from the rest of the area during the long rainy season. The group saw a lion, but otherwise made the trip safely, and invited the people to the gathering "under the trees."

James stayed at the village where his father lived rather than accompanying the boys on the rest of their rounds. He had an opportunity to spend time with his father and he was very grateful. When he rejoined the group, he talked about his father and his wisdom, and that his father "told him to live cleanly and with God."

Also later, the group told Gini that the reason James stayed back was that "if something happened to us, he would be the one to go tell the others' families," Gini related. "This impressed me. They plan for these kinds of things," Gini said.

"I'm in awe of these people."

"Majok Marier's mother walked for miles to find me where I was stay-

ing near Rumbek," Gini said. His mother was living now in Pulkar, not far from the village where Majok was when the war came, at Adut Maguen.

"Father Andrea of the Diocese of Rumbek arranged for a translator so I could talk with her. I told her if she had been standing with 100 women I would have known her, because Majok looks just like her. We talked a while; I told her Majok wanted to come, but he did not receive his travel documents in time.

"She told me she hoped Majok could come to see her soon. And then she went down the road, walking back to her village."

Gini interacted with women when she could, although she found that she was given a role of respect mostly reserved for men. In Uganda, Stephen's uncle and about 70 men gathered outside a home where they ate together, and then sat in chairs in a circle. The lights went out at 5 p.m. as power is cut every night in that area, and candles were lit. Gini was sitting among the men. She insisted on seeing where the women were.

"It might have been because it was night, and everything was by candlelight, it was such a unique scene," she said. "But I found a building next door where there were all these rooms and in each room there were women and their children. The touched me and they caressed me and we sang and prayed together. Women have a fairly subservient role there, but when things change, the women there will be amazingly powerful."

In saying farewell, Stephen's mother laid her hands on Gini and said, "You are my son's mother."

"We can share him," Gini said she told Stephen's mother.

"All of them gave them back to me," Gini said. "'You are the mother,' they told me. I took it as a compliment that they thought I was helping each of their sons."

———※———

Mama Gini, who'd recently lost her husband, also traveled with the group, which left December 26, 2005. I was so sad that I could not go. I was depressed for more than three months because of this problem of the travel documents. What made it bad was that I promised my mother I would come home in 2005. She traveled from Sudan to Uganda, like Stephen's mom. She stayed for several months with a relative in Kampala. I talked to her on the phone. She asked me when I could come home, and I did tell her that I could come in December 2005 to see her, so she was hoping to see me in person. In fact, she decided to return to the very poor village in Sudan where she was staying in order to be there to greet me. I needed my family to know that I was a person who could support them right now. I wondered what I could do to make them happy. Not going to Sudan felt like I was not a son they could depend on.

A major goal of the Lost Boys' Rumbek trip was to speak to young people in our home villages and to urge them to make good lives for themselves, to improve their communities. I wanted to be able to tell my story to the youths of Rumbek, as the group planned to do when they traveled with Gini to Sudan.

I decided I would use another method to tell the young people my story. I began writing this book, because I wanted people to know what happened, and not to forget our struggle to live despite all the animal attacks and thirst and starvation along our long journey. I wanted them to know the problems in the refugee camps. And they needed to know what our lives have been like since coming to the United States.

At the time we came here, we did not have much of a choice, as our villages were still involved in the civil war, and just as we had to leave Sudan again when Kapoeta fell to the Sudanese Army and flee across the border to Lokichoiko, we would be facing that kind of life again, and we would not get our education. That goal of education had become more important, especially as we contemplated being the main leaders of a separate South Sudan, which even back in our days in the camps looked like the only option for our area. We were told we would be able to get our educations in the United States. In fact, this was very difficult, and for me, it was not happening.

I began study at Georgia Perimeter College, and after attending for some time, I had acquired a better command of English and writing skills, but all my classes were English as a Second Language courses. No college credit applied toward a degree. It was very expensive, and my work was such that I did not have hours off to attend classes. Studying late at night—after work, after classes—was very difficult. So I stopped attending. And the goal of resettling in the United States—to receive my education—was not fulfilled. Nevertheless, I still have my goal of one day becoming a geologist so that I can find more of South Sudan's oil and other valuable resources.

As a result of Gini's and Stephen's and the others' visit to Sudan, finally someone saw my mother face-to-face! Gini met my mother, after my mother heard of her coming and she walked 15 miles one way from where she was living to meet Gini. They sat and talked for a while. Gini told her how I was doing. Then my mother got up and walked away, another 15 miles to Pulkar, the village near Adut Maguen, where I was living when the war came to my village and I fled. My mother, expecting me to be in Sudan, had left Kampala, Uganda, and traveled again several hundred miles by bus and by transport truck back to that little village in order for me to visit her and other family in our home village. So there was much disappointment all around at this missed visit.

From that time on, I began saving for travel to Sudan, and to provide some money to help my family. If my family was alive, then there were duties to that family that would require some financial resources. At the time, I was still not an American citizen, so I determined that I would not let travel documents (required by all non-citizens) hold me up from a future trip. I began studying for citizenship, which I proudly gained on August 24, 2008.

So I wrote in 2006 and 2007 all the experiences I could remember from my journey. It occurred to me also that if I wrote a book, this could help generate some funds to assist in my education goals and my other desire: to make my mother's life easier, as well as that of my village in general, by providing a deep water well so that walking miles every day to gather water for life's needs would no longer be required.

Always, my main goal has been for those who are in my home country. The writing of my story could help many of those at home and encourage them to resist the hardship they are having in their life. I understand that everyone could have some difficulties in their lives everywhere in the world. It is important to focus on any stressful situation and to be strong to get past that condition. But it is not simple for some people to endure that kind of life. Lost Boys and Lost Girls need a lot of encouragement to keep them away from depression. The Lost Boys and Girls meet together in every state they are living in to make sure stresses are relieved by conversation in groups. We love to talk in the Dinka language because we want to keep our culture in place. More than any other language in the world, it is important to know our language, and it is very helpful for Lost Boys to know our culture. I think it is useless for a person to have no culture in his or her life. Culture is the story of the country you belong to.

Some people do not think culture contributes to their lives; by culture I mean the marriage and birth and death traditions, elders' sayings, music and dance, language and stories and foods that belong to people from one place or one tribe or ethnic group. Frequently, Western people do not respect these distinctions in peoples or countries—they don't see this as important. But culture plays a big role in our lives, especially for the Lost Boys who are alive today in America and in other parts of the world where they live now. When you do not have a cultural background, I think you cannot be a good human being in other people's perception. Culture is the main thing that can prevent people from committing too much crime. Culture can help people to respect one another because people do not feel negative toward other people who share their traditions and unique way of life. Sudanese have a beautiful culture; it makes them important people when compared with other people's cultures.

We love to support one another in our culture. It is hard for Dinka people to let brothers, sisters, mothers, fathers, relatives and friends suffer in their presence. And we love to treat people equally. The Dinka are the most numerous tribe in Sudan. There are generally not Dinka in other countries in Africa. This is unusual in Africa, as tribes frequently are spread over more than one country. We could have some people in Kenya, Uganda, Ethiopia, Egypt, Libya, Chad, Central African Republic and Congo. But no, we identify with Sudan. We like to serve in Sudan and provide an environment for any tribes that are prepared to respect the rights of other tribes that also live there.

Because we are such a large tribe in Sudan, Khartoum targeted us especially when the government tried to enforce sharia law. The Dinka rose up and refused to bend to this. The Dinka see themselves as protectors of other groups also, because they are such a large group in Sudan. So the Dinka-led rebellion resulted in huge displacements of native people all over Sudan. But this was to fight the attempts of Khartoum to suppress all of our native cultures.

Nine

===

A Dinka Finds a Bride

After much saving and shopping on the Internet for a low fare—low meaning it would cost at least a couple thousand dollars, saving money to take home to my family—and gaining several months' leave from my job, I finally was able to arrange a trip to Sudan. The trip took place from early December 2008 to February 2009. I boarded the flight in Atlanta with great anticipation. On the flights over to Atlanta, there had been many novelties—bathrooms that seemed to want to flush a whole person through the bottom of the plane; unusual foods served hot in little trays; sleeping through the night with only occasional "pings" as the pilot experienced turbulence and told us to fasten seat belts, then waking up in Amsterdam—Europe.

Now I was used to many mechanical wonders of the society that I saw for the first time in 2001, especially since the flights from my home involved several different stops, and more than a couple of jet airliners. However, on my first return to Sudan since the war, my first meeting with my family in 21 years, I was able to view earth from above. Flying over the Mediterranean Sea, I could see its blue waters. I viewed Libya as we approached Africa, and then the vast desert of Darfur in western Sudan. It actually took four hours to fly over all of Sudan. From there we flew to Uganda, to Entebbe International Airport in Kampala. From Kampala, I flew to Juba, and then took a single-engine plane with a propeller to Rumbek.

I had not told them the exact time of my visit, because I did not want to again disappoint my family by not arriving when expected. My mother almost went into shock when I failed to show up the first time!

Majok's mother, Yar Chol Gueny (left), and aunts, Alek Chol Gueny (rear left with dark hat) and Achol Chol Gueny (rear right), with grandchildren in Pulkar.

So I went to the business of my eldest brother in Rumbek. Malual works for a company that delivers water to businesses and restaurants in the Rumbek area. My brother was very excited to see me! But Malual wanted to know why the family did not know when I was coming. I had to explain. His boss, the manager of his company, provided a car and driver to me to take me to my mother's village, Pulkar. My brother and my sister Lela, who was now married and living in Rumbek, rode with us.

All my family was there—my mother, my younger brother Abol, my mother's sister, other aunts, uncles, cousins, and many other people. I immediately missed my grandmother, even though she had passed 20 or more years before. She would have been proud that, despite all the tragedy and hardships of the war, I finally made it home.

My grandmother, who predicted the war with the Arabs, died before the war, but she did not die violently. She became very ill and that's how she died. So she did not become a victim of the war, although hundreds of others in our village and neighboring villages did. But there were

Majok's sister Lela's daughter Cholhok Mamer Tur in Rumbek after water-bucket bath.

numerous other relatives to meet again, or to see for the first time, as my brothers and sister all were married and had many children.

"We were looking for a little boy," one of my relatives said when I arrived. "When you left you were this high," he said, holding his hand at his waist. "Now you are tall!"

The first big change I noticed is that my brothers have satellite phones. Since there is no electricity there in the bush, they charge them by means of a generator fitted specially for satellite-phone batteries. The generator runs on gasoline that is transported from Rumbek. They use a card they pay for and load minutes to pay for the calls. The calls are very expensive, but they are the only means of communication other than traveling to another location to give news verbally.

Some changes in our area, such as the availability of the satellite phones, were required by the Comprehensive Peace Agreement that ended the civil war; it was an attempt to make up for the extreme lack of development throughout southern Sudan. The satellite service and the

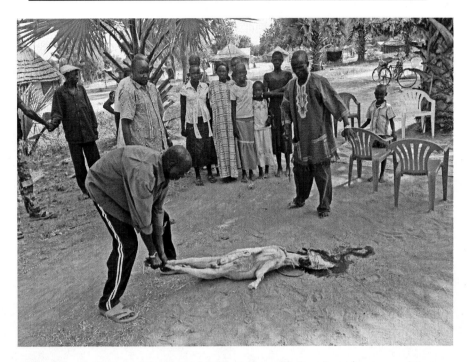

One of several goats slain upon Majok's return to Sudan. Stepping over a slain animal is a Dinka ritual to mark the return of a person long separated from his people.

water services were to be provided from Uganda and Kenya. The bottled-water service is still not in the villages, but only in the larger areas like Rumbek. So I was disappointed to see that my mother and my sister, when she was staying in Pulkar, and all the other women in the village still have to walk four to six miles one way for water.

After much rejoicing, a feast was held, and a goat was killed in my honor, as is tradition when there has been a long separation. As I stepped over the goat, I prayed for all those who did not make it home like me. There were many bodies that lay along the trail from Sudan to Ethiopia, back to Sudan and then to Kenya. Their sacrifices are why I am writing this book, and they are always with me.

I had many opportunities to tell what happened to us on our journey. My uncle, Dut Machoul Beny, was there, and he told everyone about the long walk to Ethiopia. I have not heard about his experiences in Pinyudo, as we did not see each other much once we arrived there. He had walked home when we fled Pinyudo. What he found when he arrived in Adut

Maguen was bush. Once everyone fled the village under fire during the war and relocated in other places, the brush and grasses took over. (In Sudan, if you live somewhere seven years, and then you leave it for a year, then it is no longer yours. Even if the family wanted to return after having been away for a year, they would not be able to settle at the old site of Adut Maguen. And the bush had taken over with wild growth.) So my uncle had to look further to find everyone, and he did find them in Pulkar.

There were other relatives to discuss and learn what had happened to them, like Kolnyin Nak Goljok, my mother's older sister's son, another Lost Boy, who had gone on to San Jose, California, after leaving our traveling party at JFK airport in New York City during our Kakuma-to-America flight. I told them of my conversations with him, as we talk often by phone when I am in Atlanta. He works in the evening at Home Depot there.

It did not take long for my family to let me know what my next step must be: to come back home and marry a Dinka wife. It was clear to me that I could not return home permanently at this time, as I had not yet achieved my education. But a marriage to a Dinka wife? There are many important and very old traditions with marriage in our culture, traditions that bear explaining.

In Dinka culture, the first brother gets married, and then the second, and so on. The war had interrupted the families' lives—indeed, some families were wiped out, and others continued to be dislocated all around southern Sudan. Still, the order of marriages needed to be honored, my family felt. And I was not alone among Lost Boys in learning about our families' concerns about this. Even those who had not seen their families in many years were being reminded of the obligation to the family to marry, and, before marriage, to acquire a significant bride-price to enable the marriage. So no matter what one's circumstance, this was a focus, in addition to all the other matters we were dealing with back in America. It's almost like we had gone from singing the songs we made up along our route to Ethiopia about the girl we would marry to now putting aside savings so we could look forward to that day when we sang the young girl the song as we took her as a bride.

The same year that I was reunited with my family, there were two marriages among the Lost Boys I knew in Atlanta. Among my Lost Boy friends in Atlanta, Chier Malual married a woman who was originally from his village. He met her in Kakuma Refugee camp, as she was a Lost Girl. While he resettled in Clarkston, she resettled in Australia, and they kept in touch. Judy Maves helped her with the paperwork for her entry into the United States, as the girl had an Australian passport. But she was able to come to Georgia and they married; they now live in Clarkston. Chier works for a company that supplies guttering to businesses in the area.

Bol Maliet Komu also married in 2008. He met his wife during the 2005 trip with Gini Eagen and Stephen Bayok. The girl lived in Uganda, although she was from the Equatoria region of southern Sudan, and they met when Bol traveled to Uganda. She has relocated here, so they live in Georgia as well. After working for Walmart, he now works as a security officer for his apartment complex.

Dinka men relocating to the United States will have only one wife, but in Sudan, it is traditional to have more. The reason for this historically is that the Dinka are a warrior tribe. Their numbers are important in discouraging attempts to raid their cattle or otherwise attack the Dinka. This may seem outmoded to Westerners and those not from Africa, but if you become familiar with the history of the African countries, you will see that with none of the inventions like guns and tanks that protected European countries over time, numbers of fierce warriors were the Dinka tribe's protection, just as they were for other tribal groups.

Multiple wives were seen as a way to build the force of warriors. Since a child sometimes died young or at birth, there was a need to assure having large numbers to defend the land. A young boy's training was all directed to learning how to fight with spears and shields, and practices such as the ritual scarring assured he would be brave. Large numbers of these fierce warriors is what kept the Sudd, the swamp that defines so much of the White Nile area, protected from invasions of outside forces, including the Egyptians, the British, and other groups. Additionally, the Arabic traders who eventually settled in northern Sudan were reluctant to take on these groups. In fact, a book about the Agar Dinka published in 1982 describing our people was called *Warriors of the White Nile*. So even just before the civil war broke out, we were considered warriors as well as cattle keepers.

Now, in addition to the building of a warrior force, the value of large families was that the more family, the more marriages, and the greater the number of opportunities to add to the bride-wealth of the family— if you had girls. So a series of traditional views leads to the marriages and having many children.

I went on to marry, which I will write about later, but I will only have one wife. My brothers each have two, but they live in South Sudan where that is customary. As a result of my brothers' marriages and that of my sister, I have many nieces and nephews. My elder brother, Malual Marier Maliet, now has three girls and two boys by his first wife, and two boys by his second wife. My sister, Lela Marier Maliet, has six children. My younger brother, Abol Marier Maliet, has two boys and a girl by his first wife. When I returned to Sudan in 2010, he had a second wife and two boys in addition.

So my family members were well ahead of me in the marriage area. But one does not rush into these matters. While on the 2008 trip, I told my eldest brother, Malual, to be thinking of girls who would be desirable. For the Dinka, the process of marriage is a long, well-thought-out process designed to last forever. If you have a number of girls in mind, then you need to explore one at a time, the desired girl's background, and then the families need to come to agreement on the bride-price. There are family ties to be analyzed through many conversations among many of the elders to make sure that we are not related by blood. This careful inquiry could take a long while, months at least. So while I felt this was a thing I definitely wanted to do, and I'd known it was something I would do all my life, it was not going to be quick.

The second reason it would not be quick is that there had to be significant negotiations among my family members to get their agreement to supply cows in such an arrangement. And I would need to earn money in Atlanta to pay for the cattle I would supply as my substantial part of the bride-price. A Dinka husband can count on receiving back some cattle from the bride's family after a large bride-price of cattle is made to the family—it is a present to him in honor of the marriage—but first he must make a big gift!

So my trip reunited me with my family; I got to tell them all I had been through, and I told them I had written many pages describing the journey. I was reminded more than ever of all the young people and old people, mothers and children, who had died on the way to Ethiopia. My heart was heavy every time I looked at a path through the high grasses around Pulkar. Those grasses all over South Sudan hid bodies on the route to the refugee camps. I was sad, and more resolved than ever to tell the story to as many people as I could.

I was also determined to get my life to the point where I could pursue education so I could make life better for people in Sudan. At that point, I knew we would likely be independent, and I could tell there were so many needs for this new country. I need to get the schooling that will help me make a big contribution.

And I needed to make a marriage. My family helped me see that marrying was important; the war was over, my younger brother had married before me, and that had been out of the normal order. It was time to make a marriage and to raise children who would be part of this very large Marier family, part of the very substantial clan of Agar Dinka I was a member of.

So I left Sudan to return to Georgia. My brother was going to look for girls for me to think about proposing marriage to. And I was going to have to work very hard to buy cows to make all this possible. So I flew back to Clarkston in February 2009. I would not return until I had earned enough for another round trip ticket, but more important, had raised enough money for my brother to buy my cows, my contribution to our family's bride-wealth. That was in 2010, many a long workday later.

John Garang and the SPLA

John Garang was the leader of the Sudanese Peoples' Liberation Army, the military arm of the Sudanese Peoples' Liberation Movement. The SPLA is a rebel army that fought the Second Sudanese Civil War and which is now the military force of the nation of South Sudan. The civil war displaced Majok and an estimated 4 million and killed 2 million Sudanese over the period 1983–2005.[1] *Garang was a Dinka from Bor County who had been orphaned at the age of 10 in a village in which he said no one could read. A relative paid for his education in schools in Wau and Rumbek.*[2]

He wanted to join the Anyana, rebels in Sudan's first civil war in 1962, but was convinced to go to secondary school in Tanzania. Afterwards, he received a scholarship to Grinnell College in Iowa and earned a bachelor's degree. He returned to join Anyana, and in 1972 at war's end was absorbed into the Sudanese Army. He rose to the rank of colonel and graduated from the U.S. Infantry Officers School at Fort Benning, Georgia.

Later, he took a four-year leave of absence to acquire a master's degree in agricultural economics and then a Ph.D. in economics at Iowa State University.

He defected with his men after 500 southern troops in Bor revolted over being ordered north by the Sudanese Army. He emerged two months later as head of the SPLA.[3] *During the second civil war, there was a split in the SPLA. Atrocities occurred on both sides. Riek Machar, leader of a large faction in SPLA, accused the SPLA of employing child soldiers. Their treatment and the use of the refugee camps for recruiting these soldiers has been a source of dispute.*[4]

Garang was very articulate with an excellent mastery of English and Western ideas, as well as Arabic and Dinka languages. He was interviewed by Scott Simon on National Public Radio in early 2005 just after the SPLA and Sudan completed extensive negotiations that resulted in the Comprehensive Peace Agreement that has guided relationships between Sudan and South Sudan ever since. Because a major provision of the CPA was to allow for the vote on the question of South Sudan's independence, some of Garang's comments revolved around how this very undeveloped new country would change with its new status. Speaking like the agricultural economist he was, Garang outlined ideas for development.[5]

Already, 6,000 families had changed farming practices, using hoes and plows converted from vehicles, tanks, and military equipment abandoned in the war-torn areas. Instead of humans tilling farms by hand, now the revered bulls were pulling plows. Garang said production had increased from two acres to 10 acres, "a five-fold increase per family."

He discussed other parts of a plan to build a new economy based on South Sudan's pastoralist culture:

- *Introduce new seed technologies in order to improve food supplies for families and produce surplus for market.*
- *Rather than wait for new energy technologies, use solar and wind power to bring electricity to villages.*
- *Establish small-scale dams on the many rivers in the area; electrify rural towns with 5–10 megawatt dams.*
- *Instead of building a consumerist society, as others with large oil deposits had, use oil in South Sudan to grow agriculture.*
- *Build rural towns and make them the focus of the new economy rather than creating cities that would drain the rural areas of their population.*

"We have well thought-out strategies, once peace is achieved, to use," he said. "We will use oil in southern Sudan to literally fuel agriculture. That's the only way people can benefit, especially having suffered from the past 21 years of war. We'll also avoid the rural-urban split where people from the countryside flee to the cities without the skills. They end up in slums.... So rather than to encourage people to go to towns, our policy will be to take

towns to people by building rural towns and making them focuses for development."

Garang pointed to the enormous size of Sudan as well as its offshoot, South Sudan, and characterized the challenge to build infrastructure in an area where none existed. He compared the new country's size to the area of the combined nearby countries of Kenya, Uganda, Rwanda and Burundi.

"Yet since the time of Adam and Eve, there has never been a single tarmac road in southern Sudan," he said. "So we will use the oil money to build infrastructure, to concentrate on rural development, and provide social services to our people. [We need to build roads] so that there is movement of people, goods and services and so that the domestic market functions.

"And we'll connect this with the region as well as the international community to look for markets. For the last 20 years, I've been looking for guns and bullets to fight the war; now I'll be looking for markets for our produce of our families." He asked Simon, "In the United States, what would you want? We produce the best sesame seeds. I was having breakfast at the hotel and I noted the bread had sesame seeds." He laughed, saying, "Now I'll flood America with sesame seeds. We will not use pesticides and fertilizers; this is virgin land."[6]

After the war, Garang became the first Christian and the first southern Sudanese to hold a high position in the Sudanese government. Following the Comprehensive Peace Agreement being negotiated and taking effect, Garang became vice president in the new Unity Government on July 9, 2005, and president of southern Sudan. The new nation was shocked when he died with a dozen aides in a helicopter crash on July 30, 2005. There was rioting among southern Sudanese living in Khartoum and Juba that killed 130 people.[7]

At the time of the crash, Garang was returning from Uganda where he was involved in talks with the government. The helicopter belonged to the Ugandan president, an ally of Garang in the civil war. Generally there has been no conclusion about what happened. He was replaced by Salva Kiir, who had been in the higher command structure in the SPLA.[8]

Garang's death set the stage for a strong vote for independence five and a half years later, on January 9, 2011, when the peace agreement called for southern Sudanese to decide between unity with or separation from Sudan. The vote, for which Lost Boys and other Sudanese living in the United States traveled to voting centers in several cities to cast their ballots, was overwhelmingly for creating a separate South Sudan.

A highly educated man, Garang set the tone for SPLA members to achieve education. According to Majok, SPLA was known to promote those who had schooling, and that caused the children in his villages to seek education as well. And that was a great deal of the reason they wanted to resettle in the United States.

—⚉—

Left behind in Sudan was a view of my country as it headed toward the vote for independence. Especially since the death of John Garang, I don't think anyone thought the vote could be anything but for separation. All in southern Sudan were excited about the new country. People were newly serious about doing things to build the country. I still have my goal of trying to provide a well that the people can use to pump and store water to greatly ease the life of people in the villages, where most people in southern Sudan live. There are many, many other projects that are needed to build the infrastructure for a new country.

In 2009 and 2010, I kept working as I had, and I also increased my activities with the Lost Boys in Clarkston who are Dinka. Stephen Chol Bayok is the chairman of the Rumbek community in Atlanta. I am deputy chairman. That means that any members of our community, primarily Agar Dinka tribe members, who need assistance with apartment problems, raising bail, illness and other matters go to the chairman or deputy for assistance. They in turn try to raise funds among the members, and if needed, present a request to the churches that have been so helpful to the Lost Boys and the Sudanese community.

Stephen moved out of town. After a great deal of effort, which you can read in his story included here, Stephen succeeded in gaining a bachelor's degree in management from Clayton State University. His goal was to pursue a career in teaching by getting a provisional certificate—that's a program in Georgia where teachers with bachelor's degrees other than in education can teach and work on their teaching credentials through education courses in college in the evenings.

It was difficult for Stephen to find a job in teaching, and after a lot of applications, he decided he had best earn money to make the traditional Dinka marriage. He traveled to Oklahoma to work in a meatpacking plant there. He fortunately was not in the area where they killed the animals but where they butchered and packaged cuts of meat for market. What that meant was he was no longer present in Georgia to lead the meetings and projects of the Dinka Rumbek community here. So I, the deputy, stepped in; there were many meetings where we needed to be represented, and there were activities I needed to initiate. Stephen has never lost the title of chairman; it stays with him.

I am also deputy to the chairman of another organization, the Lost Boys in Atlanta (this includes men from all tribes). The chairman is Bol Deng Bol, and I assist him.

At the same time that I was working to earn the bride-wealth and leading Lost Boys efforts, Gini Eagen introduced me to Estelle Ford-Williamson, now my coauthor, about the possibility of a book. My goal with the book was to tell our story to as many people as possible to draw attention to the problem of conflict in our country and to the problems of refugee camps. And I wanted to earn enough to build that water system back in my village and perhaps be able to go to school full time to learn geology.

My trip back to Sudan in 2010 featured my first flight on Ethiopian Air Lines. This meant that I flew into a city I'd never seen but had heard of all my life—Addis Ababa. When I was growing up, most of the trade in our part of Sudan had come from the east, from Ethiopia. At that time, there was great contact between the leader of the SPLA, John Garang, and Mengistu, the dictator of Ethiopia, so commerce between the two was strong. After the rebels deposed Mengistu, then the close association with the SPLA ceased (that's when we fled Pinyudo Refugee Camp and experienced the Gilo River massacre). Nevertheless, after the CPA, commercial contacts resumed, and on this 2010 trip, I was able to fly Ethiopian Air Lines from Dulles in Washington, D.C., to Rome for a fuel stop, and then to Addis Ababa. I then flew on to Juba and then Rumbek in the single-engine airplane. I was beginning to feel like a world traveler by this time.

On this trip to Sudan, my family had now moved again, back to my father's original village of Billing Daldiar. Even though my father had died and I don't remember him, the family is expected to know his family and to be part of his family. So that is where my younger brother is located with his wives and children. My older brother lives in Rumbek during the week, and lives in Billing Daldiar with his family on the weekend. My sister and her family live in Rumbek, although they are frequently in Billing Daldiar as well.

For sure, they were on hand to greet me again, and my elder brother, Malual, had prepared a list of girls he thought would be suitable for me. So while I visited with the family and helped in the cattle keeping, he was telling me the names of some good girls, as I had asked him to do.

Agar Dinka youth at traditional dance for New Year 2009, Rumbek area, South Sudan.

And I was considering the list. I arranged to meet each of the girls at dances and such gatherings.

I definitely had a first-choice girl, and that was Ajok. I had met her at her parents' home in the past, before I was interested in her. My brother knew her best friend, the other girl who used to go around with her. So she was not completely new to me.

Now according to Dinka custom, the suitor is not allowed to visit in the girl's home. You see her out and about in the village, often after traditional dances that go on in the evening. You ask to speak to her, and you say that you want to propose marriage to her. And then she says she will think about it. And for you to come tomorrow. What that means is, "Let's get to know each other," and "You know the process—I need to check you out, and my family needs to check you out."

So when she said she was going to think about it, that was not a commitment, but it was okay to talk to her and it meant that we were "dating," as Westerners would call it, but our culture just calls it getting to know each other. Over time, we would have walks together, but I would not go to her house, and I would not eat in her house. Everybody else could eat there, but the man seeking marriage would not eat there.

It was the duty for everyone related to me, or knowing me, to talk to her on my behalf. That's everyone's role. If my brother would go and meet her, he'd talk to her on behalf of me. When she sees one of my relatives, she is to speak to them, as she has to respect them because she is going to be one of the family. So it's not only me who goes up and talks to her, it's everybody who's close to me.

She has a right to say no, and then we go to another girl later. Also, her parents can say no. In the meantime, they will be checking out our family, and we will be checking out theirs. Good family is very important, as these villages are small and problems are known by everyone. We ask around: Do they have a lot of trouble in the family, like quarreling, separation of the parents, or the kinds of things that would mark them? If they have all those kinds of things, we will say no, we are not going to that family. You need strong family who are respectful and do the right thing. If the family doesn't work, or they are tattlers, that could end a marriage in the making. In a marriage, the groom gives a lot of cows. If you separate with the lady, you have to demand that you take your cows back. So you can see that everyone in each family has a lot invested, reputation-wise, and bride-wealth-wise, in each marriage.

I arrived in Rumbek and before too long, I talked to Ajok, and she said we could discuss it. She went to other people to check me out. Is this Majok a good person? They didn't know me as a person, but only by name, because I had been in the refugee camps for 14 years. But they knew of me, knew I was in the United States. What information they had came from my elder brother mostly. Ajok talked to other girls who were close to her, and her family asked their friends. In the several weeks long process of us getting to know each other, she held her opinions; she was encouraging, but not committing. As to the question, did I sing to her? I must confess, no. I did not sing to her. Singing is what a traditional Dinka man does for the woman he wants to marry. All those hours singing songs we made up on our long journey to Ethiopia, taking our minds off having no food, no water, and no safety—they served me well at the time. But I did talk to Ajok a great deal. Maybe she liked me because of that.

Parents like this long period of discussion because it allows them to get to know the man. They are concerned that a man may just be playing with their daughter, and they don't want that. In my case, as it was likely

Boys and girls at cattle camp near River Na'am, South Sudan, December, 2008.

my wife would live in the United States, they needed to know that I would take care of her; their greatest fear was that I would not take care of her and that we might separate in America.

The other thing, and the most important thing, that I did in Sudan is that I bought cows. I selected beautiful cows in order to make the deal of our marriage more attractive to her family. I recognized that her whole family would be involved with this; all uncles, brothers, father, mother—they all had to be satisfied with the offering of cows. Similarly, I had to go to each of my relatives to ask if they would contribute toward my bride-price. The cattle were generally kept together by our family in the cattle camp—my younger brother Abol was responsible for keeping the cattle, along with my nephews and cousins. But each cow in the herd had someone as an owner. We knew our cows by their markings, and often we decorated them with our own markings.

When I returned to Georgia, Ajok and I had an understanding that we thought we might like to marry, but the negotiation for the cows was the next step. I left this to my elder brother Malual, as he was the male head of our family, and he had done this successfully twice before, with my uncles' help. And the uncles helped him as well.

The actual cattle negotiation with the family is a three-day affair. The family of the bride comes out to the cattle camp in the morning. They have to see how many cows you have, and how many of what quality we can produce for them. My brother called me in January 2011. They were demanding that they had to have 89 cows, but my brother offered 50. They were not happy with that. They made a counter-offer of 60. I had 20 cows myself, my brother brought his seven cows, and then uncles contributed. Everyone has to contribute something, so everyone has some investment in this marriage. Then everyone else in her family, they come in the evening and everyone prepares food and eats together. In the morning our family killed a bull for them. It took a while to get the offer sealed, but the eating together and killing a bull kind of seals the deal. The gathering in the evening is where the talks continue. You hope the talks keep going and don't stop so that you can reach a settlement. It's true that in Sudan, the woman and the price that is paid for her enhances her value in Dinka culture. All this is about her value to me and my family.

As a deal is being negotiated, the cows offered and accepted are on display in the camp. Once an agreement is reached, all the other cows are released. So when people come in the evening, they can see what cows are being exchanged. When my brother told me we were still apart in the negotiations, I called other people to help. In fact, Judy Maves assisted from Atlanta by talking to a friend in Sudan whom she'd helped a great deal, and he contributed cash so I could buy two more cows!

In fact, just about the time of the marriage, the bride's family continued to negotiate with my brother, and said they would need 25 more cows. We reached agreement that we will provide these in the future. We could still marry, but they would get 25 more as our cattle herd grows in future.

Such is the Dinka way of marriage. It has worked for thousands of years, so we don't discard all of our customs at once. A big change is to take one wife. Other changes will come in future as South Sudan meets the cultures of other people, which will surely happen and has already happened with 4,000 of her sons and many daughters living in the United States.

Ten

The Beginning of
Many New Things

The year 2010 was the year I was able to plan my marriage to Ajok Mabor Malek. It was also the year that the reality of a new country of South Sudan began to take shape. While my brother was negotiating the bride-price with my in-laws-to-be, methods were being set up to provide for a popular vote among southern Sudanese for the election where we would decide whether to stay with Sudan or to form our own government.

This issue of separation was very old. When the British let go of their role in the country in 1956, the question arose whether the southern regions of Sudan should be a separate country, but that did not happen. Two civil wars had now been fought, each about 20 years long, to resolve this issue. The question would now for the first time be put to the people in the south. And the diaspora Sudanese would also take part by voting in cities in the United States. The cities were spread from Seattle to Boston, and Sudanese would travel several hours to go there.

At the end of 2010, my fellow countrymen and I were asked to register to vote in the nearest city to us, Nashville, Tennessee. This country music star–filled town is also home to many Lost Boys, and there is a very active Lost Boys Foundation there that works for the improvement of the lives of the men living there. In order to register for the Sudanese election, which was to be held in January, we traveled a month before that, on December 12, 2010. Four cars carried 18 people to Nashville from the Clarkston, Georgia, area.

Majok, Ngor Kur Mayol, with Travis Loller of the Associated Press at the historic Sudanese election in Nashville, January 9, 2011.

The voting took place at the Lost Boys Gallery, an art gallery featuring paintings, drawings, and other objects the refugees made and sold there to raise funds, a program sponsored by the Foundation. One of the highlights of this registration was that we saw about 100 Sudanese registering who were from the Rumbek area. It was like having a bit of home in Nashville.

Needless to say, there was a lot of rejoicing that we were doing this.

Taking place as it did at Christmastime, I saw the parallel between this journey and the journey that Joseph and Mary made back to his hometown of Bethlehem, to register for the census. They gave birth to the baby Jesus in that historic journey, and we were making a historic journey of our own.

A month later, on January 9, 2011, six years after the signing of the unprecedented Comprehensive Peace Agreement, the election took place in southern Sudan, and in our eight cities as well. Again we traveled to Nashville in a caravan to cast our vote. The vote was counted in Juba, which is to be the capital of the new South Sudan. We did not trust sending the ballots to Khartoum for counting. To say the least, to do so would have challenged the credibility of the vote.

On January 17, the results of the vote were announced in Juba. The vote was overwhelmingly for independence, for a country to be created six months later, beginning July 9, 2011. The nearness of this date to the American independence celebration is not lost on the South Sudanese! In Clarkston, we have celebrated this on or around July 20 so as not to be in conflict with July 4th celebrations in the United States. It is always on a weekend, to allow everyone to attend without having to worry about work schedules. These celebrations are joyful gatherings of our community, full of dancing, speeches, and foods like we have in our villages.

This second trip to Nashville was memorable for several reasons, in addition to being a historic election. One reason is that we had a film crew arranged by a nonprofit organization that supports many of our efforts. Patricia Shafer, founder and executive director of Mothering Across Continents, came with us from her home in Charlotte, North Carolina. Judy Maves, whom I've mentioned before, and Janis Sundquist, another volunteer, also accompanied us. Patricia had hired a videographer, a cinematographer, and a still photographer to accompany us in our cars. In addition, there were six vans carrying other voters. The film crew took turns riding in our cars so that they could interview different people, and then they filmed at the voting area. The videographer, Diane Estelle Vicari, had come from California, as had Ulli Bonnekamp, a noted cinematographer, so we were a little impressed with that.

The voting took place in a jubilant atmosphere. People displayed flags and sang as they stood in line—for four hours. While registration the month before had taken place over several days, this was the only day for the election on that Sunday. We got to see a lot more of our people in one place. We understand that from Georgia alone, there were 900

Sudanese—quite a large number! The weather was very cold, but we were warmed by our spirits.

When we were returning on the usually four-hour one-way trip from Nashville, it began snowing really hard at about Cartersville, Georgia. The snow kept coming down and obscuring vision, and pretty soon it was covering the road and then piling up, and the roads became slippery and congested. On the high overpass connecting I-75 South to I-285 East in north Atlanta, trying to maneuver over the very slippery and icy road, one car slid into another not part of our group, and we were stuck, along with many other cars that similarly were snowbound. Two of our four cars—the other two were either ahead of or behind this pile of cars—were totally disabled.

We were all cold and frustrated and concerned about how we would get out. Judy wore high-heeled boots. Some people had no coats. But despite it all, we were in reasonably good shape. It could have been worse.

To her credit, Patricia, who was driving one of the cars and had brought the crews for making a documentary about the voting experience, told me, "When you go with a Lost Boy, if anything happens to you, it won't be really bad."

I'm glad she had that confidence, although I didn't. Still, we had suffered far worse, that's for sure.

We called for assistance. The accident occurred about 9 at night. We waited and waited, getting colder all the time. It was about midnight when an officer finally arrived, but he said there would be no tow trucks for a long time. He suggested we move the cars ourselves. And we did. Finally we pulled out nine cars, freeing them from their icy locks. Even accident reports were handled by exchanging insurance information. We got on the road, and returned to Judy Maves' house, where we'd gathered early that morning. It was quite an end for the South Sudanese, whose country in Equatorial Africa was created that day, to be involved in such a snowstorm. And for John Manyok Anyieth, Judy's son, whose means of getting around before coming to the United States was walking, much less driving a car, to be exposed to driving in such a huge snowstorm—that was a very big deal. We've never forgotten it.

In April of 2011, I traveled to South Sudan again, this time on a Dreamliner jet owned by Ethiopian Air Lines, minus the stop in Rome. It was a direct flight from Dulles International Airport in Washington, D.C., to Addis Ababa. Every area of Africa is changing, and the significance of this much more convenient flight service is a boost for South

Sudan. It is still difficult to get to Rumbek, but it is getting easier, little by little.

This trip was to have the marriage to my wife, Ajok, to perform the traditional Dinka ceremony where the wife comes to the husband's home and stays with him. We were to be married May 23. Once I got there I arranged to buy three cows, a bull for the father, another cow for the father-in-law and a cow for the uncle-in-law. Then I needed to purchase another bull—this bull cost 1,800 Sudanese pounds, or $700 U.S. Buying it was in addition to the other cows my family and I had already supplied, and it was to celebrate the in-laws arriving at my home during our ceremony.

There would be another bull involved, but that was from my family. That is the big bull that would be slaughtered the day of Ajok coming to my house. The ceremony basically involves the girl leaving her family's home with her parents beside her and walking to my house. In this case, my home was my sister's home with her family in Rumbek. I stayed in Rumbek rather than in my father's village of Billing Daldiar in order to have access to generators powering satellite phones and Internet access. At my sister Lela's home, my people were ready to receive Ajok. The procession from her home included all the local people, and lots of girls, her

The bull that Majok bought for $700 U.S. for the wedding celebration when he married in Rumbek, May 23, 2011.

special friends. Everyone was dressed in traditional costumes, and there was lots of Dinka traditional dancing in the afternoon. According to tradition, the parents stayed at the home with us for two days, and the girls stayed at our home for seven days. And then they left.

But in the meantime, there was a lot of celebrating. We killed the bull and served the food along with the meat for two days. Then we slaughtered a goat every night the girls were there for more feasting. All this while, the traditional dances went on every afternoon from about 3 to 5 p.m. This includes the men's jump dancing, for which the Rumbek Dinka are famous, and the women's dancing that is not as exuberant but that involves traditional rhythms. People covered themselves in ashes and made the traditional body paint from natural materials and ash that cover their skin. The elaborate tattoos that are the fashion in the United States have a lot of competition from these beautiful body designs—head, feet, legs, arms, torsos—the whole body is covered.

Men dye their hair using cattle urine—it looks like the peroxide bleaching that U.S. people do. The body decoration and clothing that they wear at this time is something that has been done for centuries in my tribe. Picture books and documentaries have carried images of the lovely Dinka wedding and celebration customs over the years. We had a second celebration in Billing Daldiar in June, with a goat slain in our honor.

After the wedding, the wife does not work for three months. The girls come to her house and take care of all her duties—carrying water, gathering firewood, cooking, making clothes and fashioning gourds for cooking. All this is handled by the others for a while. She is to relax and get to know her family and her home and to create healthy conditions for a baby if that is in the works. At the end of three months, a goat is killed and a celebration is held to mark the end of that early marriage time. When she has her baby, she goes to her mother's house to have her first baby and then returns.

So that is what happened with Ajok. We had a little over six weeks as a newly married couple, and then she stayed with my sister and her family while I returned to Georgia. It was very sad to leave her after all this time of being with her.

Unfortunately, this time of return was also when South Sudan was to become independent, and there were stoppages in airline services that I hadn't anticipated. The stoppages were to keep service levels down while the transition to the new country of South Sudan took place on July 9,

2011. Everyone feared that the Khartoum government against which we'd fought for so many years would attack and not allow a peaceful transition. The small prop plane that I normally would fly from Rumbek to Juba did not fly for several days out of concern that hostilities would result in the plane being shot down. Because of this, I hired a car to take me to Juba later in July so I could connect with the flight to Addis Ababa and home.

When I did return to Georgia, I felt like a different person. I had fulfilled the Dinka tradition of taking a wife and was involved in all the ceremonies that went with that. For sure, I had more need to earn money, because I must provide for my family. I sent funds to help pay for Ajok's care, and later in 2011, I found there would be even more need: Ajok was expecting!

So in one year, a new marriage took place, a new country was born, and a new family member was on the way! I knew midwives and other women and my mother-in-law would help Ajok, but I was very concerned for her still. I came back ready to work even harder on this book so that we could have some funds to help support this new family. A complicating fact was that my work hours were less due to the worldwide recession, which affected the plumbing business a great deal. No one was building new houses, and repairs to existing homes were not being done as frequently as in the past. So my hours and earnings were less.

From Atlanta and my calls to Ajok by satellite phone, I followed the progress of her pregnancy. A midwife checked her every week. We were not sure exactly when she would deliver. At first I thought it would be February, but it turned out to be longer than that. In my country, there is not so much counting of one's months to birth, or birthdays, so much as your stage of life—a young boy, is distinguished, for instance, from a *parapuol*, one who has undergone the scarification ritual of manhood.

In April 11, 2012, Adikdik Majok Marier, a lovely little girl, was born to Ajok, who had her mother, her sister, and a midwife in attendance. She is growing every day. I have not yet been able to see her, although I talk to her on satellite phone. She recognizes Daddy or "Ba" now, and talks a little bit. I want very badly to be able to see her. However, the costs of providing for her and her mother in addition to my costs of living have made it very difficult to save for the nearly $2,500 airfare and the extra money I would need to take with me to support them and me for three months in South Sudan. Immigration processes likewise are expensive. I have not been able to find a second job that might increase the income.

Greater pressures were presented when, about a month after she was born, my daughter's umbilical cord area became infected, and she had to be treated in Rumbek. I was very worried, and I had all my friends praying for her. Most of the villages in South Sudan do not have a clinic, and the clinic in Rumbek is very basic. People must travel long distances in order to be seen by a doctor or by any medical personnel. It was decided that the baby and Ajok must go to Juba for treatment. The baby finally recovered, but my wife was diagnosed with malaria. This is a disease that often kills, but in her case she was treated with medicines and apparently is now okay.

In order to keep them near medical facilities, I arranged for Ajok and Adikdik to stay with her uncle's daughter, Anib Makur, in Juba, and so now I needed to send money for their upkeep in this town where milk and food must be purchased. In addition there are the medical visits to pay for as well as medicines. A doctor visit costs 100 Sudanese pounds, or $30 U.S. So my dream about schooling has to be just that right now while I take care of my family. I continue to visit with them frequently by phone.

Many of us among the Lost Boys find ourselves between two worlds like this. There is our new home in America, which is not new anymore, but we still have lots to learn. We have our home in South Sudan. It is not to our liking to be in two places, but we feel we do not have many choices. Our employment here benefits our communities in South Sudan and makes our marriages possible. We also feel we are contributing to America. In my case, I help make many Atlanta and Decatur homes functional for their residents through M. Cary and Daughters Plumbing Company, "The Old House Specialists." The know-how I have gained here will someday help my communities in South Sudan.

Many of the Lost Boys have not found the education they came here for—yet. There have been many obstacles, mostly financial, as higher education has continued to become more and more expensive. And there are doors that remain closed once you have the education. Stephen Chol Bayok will return from his new marriage in South Sudan to look for a job in education again. He hopes to eventually start schools in South Sudan, as the Arab-language schools that Khartoum did provide will not be available anymore. I continue to seek funds so I can go to school full-time and study geology to explore more of South Sudan's many mineral and oil resources.

My family in South Sudan helps me by encouraging me and being proud of my accomplishments. One day, my wife and daughter will be here, but just as it took a long time to reach Ethiopia, the journey to have them join me will be long perhaps, but there will be an end. In the meantime, the changes to South Sudan that need to occur will take some time and there will be bumps in the trail along the way, but we will get there. The tall grasses that line the paths we took to Ethiopia still hold the remains of the many who did not make it. For them we will drill water wells and build schools and clinics and improve South Sudan's infrastructure so we will no longer be mistreated by the north and other parts of the world that think we are not a good people. It will be our knowledge and sacrifices in the name of those who did not make it that help South Sudan thrive.

Eleven

Stories of South Sudan

As I wrote about the journey and reflected on what happened there, I was reminded of some of the people who were with us and the stories we told during our difficult times. I have spoken of my mother's mother's brother, my uncle, Dut Machoul. There was another relative with us also, Kau. The things that Kau and Dut did for us during these times of near starvation and thirst and animal or enemy attacks show the way our people care for each other, and that is good to know.

As I mentioned, Dut found me first, and then we found my cousin Kau, who is my cousin on my mother's side, so he is also related to Dut. The three of us, Dut, Kau, and I, walked for a while, and then the boys Laat and Matoc joined us after we heard them on the path speaking our dialect. So Dut and Kau did a lot of things. When Dut was not going to be around, Kau could take care of me.

Each night I slept between Dut and Kau; just as in our village, we slept side by side, boys in one area, girls in another. This was for safety. In the night, if something happened, I could not just wake up and run away; someone needed to know. I had to wait until they actually knew the way to go and then I could follow. I was told, "If you are in the night and you hear something, you have to find us."

The older guys, Dut and Kau, looked out for me and they looked out for Matoc and Laat. Matoc was a little older than me, and Laat was near the same age. That is our culture. If you have a child and the child is young, parents look out for him. But if you grow up to be older, you can be responsible for anybody. You can defend people. That's what happened for us. People would see children going by themselves. There would be groups, and they would have an obligation to help them. As I said, very often our parents and grandparents were training us to survive, to be able to do for ourselves, if something happened to them.

If the parents are gone, older sisters may be in charge. When we were at home, some soldiers or animals or illness could come, and the parents could die, or the mother could die in childbirth. Someone would be responsible—a brother, a sister, or a grandmother. Now if anything happens, you have to make a life like other people who know their parents. The people in our country never know what may happen. If you don't train your children to be strong, they won't survive. So that is part of our culture.

When we boiled the sorghum, that's what we ate, and the two of them—Dut and Kau—were the ones to do the cooking. We might gather three stones on which to perch the cooking pot over the fire. We would be allowed only to put some grain in the gourd for them to cook. But otherwise, they cooked for us. (Only later at the refugee camps did we cook for ourselves.) For three months, when we were in Poktub, the only place we were able to stay for a while because we bartered for food, we ate sorghum grain, cooked. The rest of the journey, when it came time to cook something, Kau and Dut would do this. We didn't cook that often, because we had nothing to boil. But when we did, it would be during the day because a fire at night would give us away to the enemies. We kept grain boiled during the day in our gourds and ate from it at night.

Walking barefoot at night, Dut and Kau would guide us. They did many things to take care of us. Later when we were in the camps, we were separated. I did not see Kau at all. Maybe he went back to Sudan while we were in Pinyudo. I did see Dut once before the camp collapsed and he went back to our home village at Adut Maguen—actually the new village nearby, as our original village was destroyed.

When we first came to Pinyudo and for about the first six months, things were very hard at the camp—people were dying of starvation and disease after their long journeys—and the camp was just getting set up by the UNHCR. Then about May to June of that year, 1988, everything was changing. You could get a blanket and share it with another guy. So I saw Dut, and I gave him a blanket.

Besides the responsibility to care for younger children, another thing in our culture is shared stories; at Pinyudo, during the evening hours we would tell the stories like our grandmother would tell us. The stories would help us to be close to our families. And it would take our minds off the fact that we had no food. The really skilled people were the ones who could narrate where they are from and who their people are. For instance, I could tell about my father's name and my grandfather's, all the way back to seven generations. Then I could do the same on my mother's side. And then someone else would tell about their family names. After that, people would know you, and sometimes someone would come to me and say, "So and so is close to you; he is one of your relatives," because he would recognize the names.

It helps in marriages because you cannot marry your cousin, so people need to know who your family are; in fact, marriages cannot be negotiated until family members and older people in the villages are consulted in great detail while a marriage is being proposed to determine who are the family of the proposed bride and groom so that cousins will not marry cousins. Sometimes mothers don't have time to discuss your relatives, but a grandmother can tell you these stories and these family members' names.

We had these community gatherings in the evening at Pinyudo and also at Kakuma. Agar and Malual and Cic—all Dinka tribes—would meet in their own groups. Agar have ways that are different from Malual and Cic communities. We would tell these stories in these gatherings. We have some common stories, such as Lion stories and Fox and Hyena.

In the story of Fox and Hyena, Fox is the one that is always cheating everybody. The one who gets fooled is Hyena. Fox would say to Hyena that he was going to take Hyena to a bee hive and let him get the honey out. But the Hyena says, "I see you Fox—today, I'm going to eat you because you fool me every time."

So the Fox shows him some honey and he tastes it and he says, "What is that?" Fox says, "If I show you, you are going to eat me."

And Hyena says, "No, I won't eat you."

So Fox took the Hyena up there in a tree and he tied Hyena up near the honey cone. Our people have a way to help the bees make and keep the honey. It's a cone, with one side open. It's a long cone, made out of bamboo. They make it like a box, and it has holes on each end. Then they just hook a noose on one and they have a little box and a way to retrieve it. They find a tree with two branches coming to a Y to sit the box between, so the bees can go in there and make honey. So they had to tie the Hyena to the tree.

"I'm going to tie you up here and then you can eat all the honey you want, and then I'm going to come back," Fox tells him. He ties him up and says, "Don't touch the box. Now I'm going away from here." When the Hyena puts his hand in there all the bees sting him and he just cries. That's a story that we tell.

Another story we tell in our area because we have a lot of lions who attack and eat people.

There are some people in Rumbek—they are not Agar Dinka, they are another tribe, so we Dinka often get confused with them—who are believed to be lions as well. In the day they are persons. At night they turn into lions. So they are going to eat people. People say, "That is not going to happen because you can't turn a human into a lion."

So there's a guy who has a bull, a very nice bull. So what happened is, this guy followed him everywhere. He followed the bull owner into the forest and asked him:

"Do you know this place?"

"Yes," the man said. "I graze my bull here." The man who was following him then knew he might have neighbors nearby, and if he called out, they would come running, so he did nothing. They moved to another area in the forest.

"Do you know this place?"

"Yes, I know this place. This where I had my cattle last year."

Woman straps hand-made pots onto bamboo sled to take to market. Note cloth for carrying pot on head at left.

"Do you know this place?" the second man would ask at the next site.

"No, I don't know this place." Then the person/lion said, "Just wait here."

He then ran to the other side of the bush. He hit his head on a tree, and he turned into a lion. So he came back and attacked and ate the man.

There are many mistaken beliefs about people in our part of South Sudan being part lion. When you go to northern Bahr El Ghazal province and say, "I'm from the Agar Dinka," people think you are a lion. The impression that they have, because the lions bring trouble to their area, is that we are lions. Most of the people laugh about us. They say, "These people are part lion. So during the day they will be people, but at night they will go and turn into lions."

In fact, there is a group, a tribe, not Agar Dinka, but they reside in the Lakes State, and I think that is why we get confused with them: We are in the same state. So people think of Rumbek, they think the lion people. In fact, these people, called Malual Aguek Bar, are 100 miles from Rumbek. But we all, Agar Dinka and these Malual Aguek Bar people, live in the same state. Our province, Lake Province, became Lake State after independence. There are other small tribes, like Cic Dinka, like the Atot tribe, and Gok Dinka—these people are close to Rumbek and when they go to different areas, people call them Agar, but they are not Agar. They are different groups within our state. So there is confusion about the Agar and these lion people.

These Malual Aguek Bar people—they live near Yirol—they do believe they are part lion, that they have a relationship with a lion in their ancestors. They think they have special powers over the lion, and that when a lion comes, it will not eat their people. They worship lions sometimes. They say that, if a lion comes around, they can make a sacrifice, and the lion will just turn away.

In our groups in Pachala and Kakuma, we heard people say "You (Agar) are the lions, the people who turn into a lion at night."

We told them: "You know what, if you go to the whole of Sudan, we are the people who build the tall buildings more than anyone in southern Sudan, all of Sudan, because of the lions. If we are lions, why do we build these tall houses because the lions eat us?" We laughed about the fact the others thought we were the lion people.

So what we were saying is, it's not true. Also, it doesn't happen. How can someone turn into a different animal? How do you put that big hair on your head, or how do you get all these claws and they go back in? How do you change all those things at the same time, and then return to a human being? That's what people actually believed; people who had not been to our area believed it was true. We believed the same thing of the people from Malual Aguek Bar tribe, that they are close to the lion.

When we came together in the camps, people began finding that what they thought about us is not true, that it went back to the Malual Aguek Bar people, who believe they have a special tie with the lion. You cannot be human and an animal. Nothing happens like that.

When I was seven and fleeing my home, and we were three days from my village, in Pankar where the lion attacked us, I thought about the stories I knew about lions. We were downstairs on the ground and we were crying, and the people who were up above were laughing about those crying under the house, and I was thinking, these people may be close to these animals. Maybe one of them has returned to the animal, and is making that sound, the roar of the lion we heard. Later, we went upstairs to sleep, as the people realized there was danger in our sleeping below. So I guess I decided they were not part lion after all, as I slept upstairs near them.

And there is the story we learned about a guy called Anyeth Makou. When this man appears in the village, people say he comes with the lions, so children should be up in their house at night. (Often people sleep under the house at night because it is cooler in hot weather.) When you hear anything at night, then just be quiet, and sit there. Don't do anything to call attention to where you are. When we were children, there was no arguing with this. If Anyeth Makou was around, you went upstairs!

The other thing that we believed of the Malual Aguek Bar people when we thought they ate people is that they were animals who might survive death. When one of them died, they had to bury that person deep and sit there and pound on the grave for seven days so that he wouldn't jump out of the grave. People told terrible stories about this, and most credited the Agar Dinka, but it was this other group. All these stories they told to keep people in fear. But many people still believe them. If I go up to northern Bahr el Ghazal, they will say, "You are people who eat people."

However, in our groups, people began finding that what they said about us is not true. In fact, many nights we told these stories, and we laughed as we heard what people thought we were. Such laughing and joking took our minds off our empty stomachs, as there were many nights like that, when we were very hungry. We came to see that these stories were made up mostly, that the lion-person was a myth, probably created to make us fear other people; if our parents made us fearful of people who were part lion, maybe we would not stray into areas where we would be unwelcome or unsafe. Or if children made a fuss about sleeping upstairs when parents felt they should, word that Anyeth Makou was in the area and the lions came with him might inspire a child to seek the higher place at night.

Through the refugee camps, we got to know ourselves, our area, and our people; we got to know other tribes, as we met with them in groups, and played sports and went to school together. And we walked to different areas in Sudan. We went to the Nuer area, we went to Murle area. We went to the Taposa area; we went to Central Equatoria, where they had different tribes—Acholi, Madi, Zande. These are tribes that are near Kapoeta. So we got to know areas that were not our own, and people got to know us.

A Story of Our Leaving Kakuma

Our resettlement and the way it was handled among our people tells a story of the special obligation we Dinka—and the other Lost Boys—feel for supporting those back home. It shows how bound we are to our home, even though we are citizens here and we contribute here and we are Americans in every sense. Yet we are also people with two countries. The decision to leave shows that.

The UNHCR came to the unaccompanied minors group that was going to turn out to be the Lost Boys group. Radda Barnen, the Swedish group that is known in the United States as the Save the Children Foundation, was working with the Lost Boys group, and they and our teachers were involved in the decision about this. They had a lot of questions. How would it affect the boys? What about the new culture? It would be good for us to get an education and establish our lives. They were concerned about this, because if we came here and had a new life and a new culture, they worried it would not work well for the goal of seeing us do something that would be positive for our country. Finally, they decided that it would work if we came to America and then went back and helped people when things got settled in the war. Remember, at this time, it was 2000, and we were far from a peace settlement with northern Sudan.

So they went over with us the negative parts and the positive parts of this decision. They were thinking we could go to school. We could go back and teach other people in South Sudan, or do the jobs that would be needed to establish the systems in the new country. And they were worried that we were young. When we came to the American culture, we might turn in different ways—many would go to drink a lot, and that is not good in our culture; it was against our culture. And it is bad because all our people when they are drinking and drinking, they end up alcoholic. Those were the things they were worried about because drinking was not the thing in our culture.

The elders in the camp advised a lot of people. Any group of people that was leaving, they called them in, and they made a ceremony. They bought a goat or cow and they slaughtered it and the whole group would come and then they would talk to them. These were not relatives necessarily, but older people in their communities in the camps. The elders each gave something he thought the person could get from the United States. Each elder talked. Those leaving had to listen. That's the tradition during one of these ceremonies. They warned us about drinking, looking for women, forming gangs, and going to drugs. If you are not from that country, don't take the bad things from that country that will spoil your life, they said. Look for what you are going for. If you go to school, go to school that you choose. If you are working, make money and then do something in your life. So that is the advice that they gave to each of the Lost Boys.

They knew that if you go to a different culture or a different place, you have a lot of problems fitting in. They wanted to warn us about that, but then they told us we should go, and we could come back to our country: "You have to remember us and don't forget our country."

"And don't forget your people," they said. Then when we would have our community group, the elder would call our name; then we would come and talk to him, and he would give a blessing that nothing would get in our way, and we would be free, and he would say, "Don't forget about us, and we want you to come back."

And that's why people who have resettled here work hard and supply a lot of people with money so they can treat those who are sick in their families. And those who have resettled do a lot of other things, and they keep talking to their families, and they advise them and see how they are doing. And they also help them.

We who have come here try to tell people what is going on in Sudan.

We have spoken before people in churches, in school, and among coworkers at our employers' businesses. Many people thought the war was going on still, that the war kept going and going, and that people still were dying. So when it stopped in 2005 and the Comprehensive Peace Agreement was signed, we felt we needed to tell people about it. So we did a lot of speaking to groups, and we still do, to educate people about our country. Even though there is peace there is still a great deal to do.

Living in Two Worlds

There have been a tremendous number of success stories of the Lost Boys coming to this country, and there have been some difficulties. Without a doubt, we feel there have been strong successes; many have completed advanced education, most are well employed in fields of work that needed assistance: plumbing old houses and assisting in renovating others, working in the processing plants, being distributors of building materials, working in South Sudan in new areas of infrastructure development. Even some of our group in other cities and other parts of the world that I'll describe later have become actors or models. But there has been sadness along the way also.

The commitment to one's people includes making a traditional marriage. This continues no matter what the hardships people endure, and no matter how long the separation from the intended wife. There are many of my friends whose stories are like mine—we work very hard to earn money for cows to pay the bride-prices for our wives, and then we have to wait a very long time to be able to live in the same country, whether in America or in South Sudan or elsewhere. Mostly this is due to the fact that we have to continue to pay for cows purchased, or we have to provide money now for the wife's and family's upkeep in Sudan. In addition, if we hope to bring a wife and family here there is an immigration fee close to the cost of the very expensive plane ticket, around $2,400! So that is the bind that young men such as myself find ourselves in. We do not complain, as the process of creating a Dinka family is our tradition, and we want our wives and families to reflect these values. But it does provide a source of stress for us—for family back in Sudan as well as for the young men here.

Probably no story shows this as much as that of Elder Ber Yuot; he had to wait quite a number of years to get married and live in the same area. Ber actually preceded us to Atlanta. He was here when we arrived, and we met him after Cyndie Heiskell discovered our poor living situation at Kensington Manor and got us moved to a better apartment after our arrival in the winter of 2001. Cyndie worked on our behalf and convinced one of the refugee services organizations to employ people to help us who can talk to us, as there was no Sudanese in that role before. So he worked for one of those organizations, I believe with the Episcopal Church.

We called him "Elder Ber" because he was older than us, and he helped us with every kind of thing. Anytime people needed to move, he would help them. Anytime you come to a new culture and a person has been there and he is one of your people, it helps a lot when you need help.

Ber had been relating to the woman who became his wife when we first knew him, so that was 2001. He had actually come to the United States from Egypt, so he was not a Lost Boy, but he was Dinka fleeing the regime while living in Khartoum, in the north. During the civil war, southern Sudanese people who had moved north were under attack also, but in a different way. The Sudanese government actually took the southerners who were in Khartoum and put them outside in a camp in the desert. The camp was called Jabrona. The government said they were supporting the rebels; that was their justification for rounding people up and sending them to the camp. Anyone who had a name that sounded Dinka or Nuer was accused of being SPLA, of supporting the rebels. They moved them from the city and took them out to the desert. So our people in the north were suffering, especially the Dinka and Nuer tribes as they are the largest in southern Sudan, and so these people were in a terrible situation. If they stayed, they would be incarcerated in these camps.

So Ber fled from Khartoum to Egypt. He made his own way to the United States through the immigration process. Other Sudanese were coming to the United States from Iraq, Libya, Lebanon, or Syria. They went to Egypt and these other countries because they were forced to leave the country of Sudan or be held in this desert camp. Ber and his fiancée had their marriage plans delayed until they could be here together. She stayed in Egypt while he came here. So they had this long-distance relationship. Finally, after a number of years working in refugee services, he joined the U.S. Army, and then he went to Egypt in 2008 or 2009, and they married there a year later. So finally they were married and they were closer to coming here together. But, since he was in the army, he was deployed to Iraq. And he died in a bomb blast two days after he arrived.

So these Dinka marriages still occur, but they have to await many other circumstances—immigration papers, the husband having enough money to support himself, send money home to family, pay for family illnesses, support the wife and children, pay fees to immigration and heavy airline fares. There are many obstacles. But as many of us live in community, we work hard, and we support each other. And we keep focused on why we are here—helping our country.

Twelve

Celebrities and Friends of South Sudan

There were a few people who came forward to help the refugees and to publicly draw attention to our desperate conditions during the Second Civil War that ended in 2005—and since then. Possibly the most prominent of these was Manute Bol, the National Basketball Association player and fellow tribesman from southern Sudan. Manute was an extremely tall figure in basketball as well as to our Dinka people, to the refugees, and to the cause of an independent South Sudan.

What I remember about Manute is that he saved people's lives when we fled Ethiopia during the overthrow of the SPLA rebels' friend, Mengistu, the Communist dictator of Ethiopia. Southern Sudanese refugees had been shot dead in the Gilo River as they fled the camp at Pinyudo. When they finally made it back to a relatively safe area of southern Sudan that was in SPLA hands, Pachala, the refugees were massing outside the town, but did not have food or water. The UN had trouble trying to get food supplies to the refugees.

But Manute chartered an airplane to bring us food. He came himself to Pachala to see to its delivery. I did not see him that time, but I saw him later when he came to Kakuma Refugee Camp during the famine and poor food supplies in 1993 or 1994.

And then later, after I resettled in the United States, I attended a wedding of a fellow Dinka where he was also a guest, in Richmond, Virginia. Manute shared the table where we ate at a dinner the night before the wedding. He was very impressive. I remember that he asked the bride what she would like for a present. She said she'd like a plasma screen TV.

"That's just a small thing," Manute told her. "That is nothing. I thought you wanted something big, like a car." Manute was used to donating to his country in a big way. He gave everything that he had, leaving little for himself.

The people of South Sudan are richer for the life of Manute Bol, and certainly South Sudan might not exist without his contributions.

—ɷ—

Manute was seven feet, seven inches tall; he played for the Washington Bullets, after being selected in the second round of the 1985 draft. He then played two years for the Golden State Warriors and then the Philadelphia 76ers for three seasons, and returned to Philadelphia after playing for other NBA teams.[1]

Manute's main advantage was his ability to block and discourage the opposition by his sheer size. According to Phil Jasner, Philadelphia Inquirer *sports writer, Manute blocked an average of five shots a game as a rookie, and later, in one half, he knocked back 11 shots, eight of those in one quarter.*[2]

"And amazingly, he loved taking threes," Jasner wrote. "He was an astounding 20-for-91 with the warriors in '88–89, and playing for the Sixers in '92–93 knocked down six of 12 in the second half of a loss to the Phoenix Suns. He finished his career with 1599 points, 2,647 rebounds and 2,086 blocks."[3]

Jasner went on: "Bol would donate virtually all of his salary to the rebel movement in Sudan, and to feed the hungry there. He would make personal appearances, then donate the fees. He beat the Chicago Bears' legendary Williams "Refrigerator" Perry in a celebrity boxing bout." He even contracted for one day with an Indianapolis minor league hockey team even though he was unable to skate.[4]

Writer Alan Sharavsky said reports were that Manute donated $3.5 million to Sudanese causes along with "endless time and effort which I witnessed first hand." Manute died of kidney problems and Stevens-Johnson syndrome in Charlottesville, Virginia. It was believed Bol fell victim to the skin disease after either taking kidney medication in Africa, or delaying treatment for the kidney condition while he was in South Sudan. He was there helping construct a school as part of his Sudan Sunrise charity and had been convinced to extend his stay until after the Sudanese elections. On his way back from southern Sudan, he'd stopped in Dulles, Virginia, and he was hospitalized in Charlottesville, where he succumbed.[5]

Bol was known for his practical jokes and his sense of humor. Once, he jumped center against Mark Eaton, of the Utah Jazz—who is 7 feet, 4 inches. Eaton told him, "Man you are big!"

"No, mon," Bol told him with characteristic Dinka inflections, "You are big, I am just tall."[6]

The Associated Press carried the story of Bol's funeral at the Gothic National Cathedral in Washington, D.C., where 100 mourners gathered and the Republican senator from Kansas, Sam Brownback, eulogized him:

"I can't think of a person I know of in the world who used their celebrity status for a greater good than what Manute Bol did. He used it for his people. He gave his life for his people."[7]

According to the AP, Bol lost some 250 members in the Sudanese civil war. He was buried in his home village of Turalei in Warab State of South Sudan, where he wanted to be buried, next to his grandfather. It was a long trip back. His casket arrived in Juba, South Sudan, on one day; the next, his family accompanied the body aboard a two-hour flight, followed by a four-hour road trip through the relatively unpopulated area.[8]

"Hundreds of people from surrounding villages walked to Turalei for the burial and lined the road from outside the settlement right up to his family's mud-walled hut," Reuters reported. "Young men carried pictures of the sports star and a local basketball team accompanied the coffin that was lowered into the grave lined with cattle hides." The ritual slaughtering of bulls—a high tribute—would continue for the next two or three days.[9]

Manute Bol's effects would long be felt in U.S. basketball. Shortly after his death, a young man from his home town who was a Lost Boy was playing basketball in New York, at a Lutheran international exchange school. Ring Ayoel followed Manute's example in immigrating to the United States to use his size to advantage in basketball. A 7-foot-4 center, together with three other young men from Sudan, also very tall, caused the exchange school to have the tallest team in basketball.[10]

—m—

Currently, there is another NBA player from South Sudan, Luol Deng, and he learned basketball from Manute. He is also from the Dinka tribe; so he is one of my tribe. He plays for the Chicago Bulls, and he is active in charities to bring education and sports to refugees in camps. We in South Sudan are proud that he is reaching back to those in the camps; he knows how hard it is to be a refugee and seek asylum in another part of the world.

During the 2012 London Olympics, the world learned of a man who ran without his country's sponsorship, because he refused to acknowledge the country whose flag he could have run under. That country was Sudan, from which we became independent in 2011. South Sudan was his country, but it did not have the resources to create an Olympic committee, so it could not sponsor him. So he ran under the flag of the Olympics. His name is Guor Marial, and I got a chance to meet him—I actually arranged for him to speak at a fundraiser, making contacts so that he could come to Atlanta in 2012.

As deputy chair of the Rumbek Sudanese Community (Stephen Chol Bayok, the chair, was working in Oklahoma at the time), I was asked to arrange for him to come to Atlanta by those who were helping another Lost Boy, King Deng, or Makur Abior, to publicize his book, *The Original Lost Boy*. The event was for the King Deng Foundation, which assists street children in Lakes State and plans to start a school for them. Guor was from another Dinka tribe, the Agok Dinka from the Unity State, near the northern border with Sudan. As it happened, I knew someone who knew him, and we were able to arrange Guor's visit. He came from Arizona where he was training for the race. His schedule was extremely tight, but because of his commitment to help his people, he agreed to come and speak and help raise funds for these children to be educated.

I really respect people who take a stand and refuse based on memories of the war to embrace the old country too quickly. One day, things may be different, but for now it seems right to maintain a separate identity. That is what so many, many people died for.

Another person who has raised the visibility of the South Sudanese people is Alek Wek, a supermodel who also was a refugee, who after many years made her way to London and eventually hit it big in the media. She has also championed the cause of refugees in South Sudan.

Alek Wek has represented many fabled houses of fashion such as Christian Dior and Diane Von Furstenberg, and has published a memoir of her life as a refugee who fled southern Sudan after the civil war broke out and destroyed their village. She was sent to Khartoum and her family followed after. Her father, in the long walk from South Sudan, developed a hip fracture, and died of complications from surgery after he made it to Khartoum. Alek and some of her family of nine siblings fled to London, and the others were eventually given refuge in Australia and Canada.[11]

In London Alek worked outside school hours and sent money to her mother back in Sudan, finished school, and enrolled in fashion technology and business at London College of Fashion, a top school. HELLO! *Online states that she became "one of the hottest new faces on the scene," and pretty soon the top design houses were after her to wear their fashions on all the runways. "Her distinctive looks, so different from the usual catwalk face, caused a stir in the world of fashion and garnered a raft of awards, including 'Best New Model' at the Venus de la Mode Fashion Awards, 1997 MTV model of the year and 'Model of the Decade' from* i-D.[12]

Alek is very active in advocating for the plight of the refugees, and is in fact a member of the U.S. Committee for Refugees Advisory Council, where she tries to bring attention to the plight of the humanitarian disaster in Sudan and other places.[13]

Friends of the South Sudanese

Some well-known celebrities from the United States and other countries have come forth in support of South Sudan since the area's plight became more widely known. In turn, Hollywood has responded by recognizing the artistic gifts these men and women have brought to the United States and the Western world. In 2003, Bruce Willis' movie Tears of the Sun, *featured some of the Lost Boys, the refugees from southern Sudan, portraying the west Africans in a story about rescuing a doctor who won't go until her 70 refugees go with her. Other Lost Boys have become known as actors, including Alphonsian Deng, who goes by Alepho Deng, and Benjamin Ajak. Both of them were in* Master and Commander: On the Far Side of the World *with Russell Crowe, where they learned how to sail a tall ship. Alepho has had other roles as well.*[14]

Alepho's brother, Benson Deng, and their cousin, Benjamin Ajak, together with Judy Bernstein, wrote a book, They Poured Fire on Us from the Sky, *a very popular story of the journey each of them made across Sudan, some of them to Ethiopia, and then all eventually to Kenya. The story is told as each of them experienced his journey. All three ended up in Kakuma Refugee Camp, and after a number of years they were selected for the resettlement program and boarded a plane destined for points north, and to the United States and San Diego.*[15]

Two others who have brought their celebrity to the causes of the South Sudanese are Ger Duany, a former child soldier in the Sudanese civil war and now noted actor and model, and Emmanuel Jal, former child soldier and now actor, hip-hop star, and celebrated activist who brings a message of peace through his music. Ger was forcefully recruited into the war as a seven-year-old and escaped at the age of 14, making his way to camps in Ethiopia and Kenya. He got a role in a film, I Heart Huckabees, *when the director sought a real refugee to play the role of one; he has subsequently developed more roles in feature films, enjoyed a career as a model, and starred in a documentary about the South Sudan independence election in 2011,* Ger: To Be Separate. *Jal has acted in movies, but is best known for his appearances and music recordings. Both Ger and Jal will be in a feature film soon to be released, a fictional story that draws on Lost Boys' experiences.*[16]

Actor and activist George Clooney has had the highest profile among those non–South Sudanese advocating for the country's needs. He was pictured on the cover of Newsweek *in February 2011, just after the independence election in South Sudan and areas of the South Sudanese diaspora. The article highlighted the unique role that celebrity activists such as Clooney, Bono, Brad Pitt, and Angelina Jolie play in Africa and other countries. Their goal is to raise awareness of world problems that might otherwise receive little or no attention in the press.*[17]

"Clooney had traveled to the oil-rich contested region of Abyei on the eve of South Sudan's historic referendum," John Avlon wrote in the Newsweek *article after he accompanied Clooney. "When the polls closed seven days later, Africa's largest nation would be divided into two separate countries by electoral mandate." After a war that took 2 million lives, it seemed incredible that such a peaceful election took place. Most of the credit belonged to the resolve of the southern Sudanese civilians and military who had fought the war. But in assuring the rest of the world would be watching in a very public way, "Clooney played a pivotal role."*[18]

Clooney was not known in this part of Africa for his movies—there are few movie houses—but for his visits to South Sudan, many with the cofounder of the Enough Project, John Prendergast. "Amid the factions, Clooney is seen as a man unconstrained by bureaucracy, with access to power and the ability to amplify a village's voice onto the world stage," the Newsweek *article said.*[19]

The teaming with the Enough Project enabled Clooney to link with an ongoing organization dedicated to ending genocide across the world. The Project brings attention to areas of mass human suffering, the sites of the world's worst atrocities.[20]

The son of a journalist (his father Nick Clooney, 78, George, and a couple of congressmen were jailed briefly after a demonstration at the Sudanese embassy in Washington in 2012), Clooney has focused attention on this particular country with an awareness of how the media that follow him so relentlessly can be turned to help the cause of observing and action on behalf of countries such as South Sudan.[21]

"Celebrity can help focus news media where they have abdicated their responsibility," he told Avlon. While he can't change the media, he said he can use it to help influence politicians to do something concrete. The paparazzi? "If they're going to follow me anyway, let them follow me here (to South Sudan)." And they have. If not the paparazzi, then the media in general pay attention to Clooney's statements.[22]

"He has briefed the Senate Foreign Relations committee and the UN Security Council," the article states. He and Barack Obama "first worked together on Darfur. After their first Oval Office meeting, Obama appointed a special envoy to Sudan. The second meeting ... resulted in the deployment of [then] Sen. John Kerry to Khartoum."[23]

In the fall of October 2010, just before the January 9 referendum on independence, there was question among diplomats and those in South Sudan whether the election might even happen. (The 21-year war just ended had followed another such long war, the First Sudan Civil War.) Clooney's impact cannot be overstated, as Salva Kiir, who took the provisional government's leadership after John Garang died in the air crash, had effectively kept the South Sudan coalition together. The Obama administration and the UN focused their attention on the issues at that time. "And China— Sudan's largest oil investor—changed the equation by belatedly announcing it would support the referendum.[24]

"Still, after Clooney launched a media blitz to mark 100 days to the referendum, English-language newspaper, magazine, and website mentions of the Sudan referendum spiked from six to 165 in one month. Between October and January, the referendum was mentioned in 96 stories across the networks and cable news—with Clooney used as a hook one third of the time. In that same period, 95,000 people sent emails to the White House demanding action on South Sudan. Valentino Achak Deng, the former 'lost boy' known to Americans as the subject of a bestselling 'fictionalized memoir' by Dave Eggers, What Is the What, *says simply: 'The referendum would not have taken place without his involvement. Never. He saved millions of lives. I don't think he knows this.'"*[25]

Clooney has joined his emphasis on media with his concern for South Sudan by beginning the Satellite Sentinel Program. This program, which is carried out with Prendergrast's organization, the Enough Project, provides the services of satellite surveillance to pinpoint areas of conflict between Sudan and South Sudan and between Sudan and Darfur. Once documenting areas where there are military attacks, he raises concerns in the media to focus attention on the issue.[26]

The attacks of the Sudanese government's Sudan Army Forces (SAF) in Darfur and adjacent areas have become a focus. Conflicts have centered on the Sudanese Liberation Army (SLA), a rebel group in Darfur created in the style of the SPLA. The SLA has joined with the Justice and Equality Movement and formed the Sudanese Revolutionary Front (SRF) in its efforts to end the Bashir regime and form a democratic, secular government, in opposition to the Islamist-focused government that has been in power for so many decades.[27]

Clooney's Satellite Sentinel Program found that both Khartoum's Sudan government and the SRF were occupying areas of Kordofan state, an area that was supposed to be demilitarized. The satellites further showed craters in the market and adjoining neighborhoods near Abu Korshula in Southern Kordofan state, a sign that Sudanese government aircraft had bombed the area in an effort to dislodge the rebels. The Sentinel Project called for all forces, government and rebel, to withdraw and observe peace.[28]

While the satellites were able to pick up the images of war and occupation, the UN, which was charged with keeping the peace in the area, was unable to physically access the areas in Southern Kordofan, so they had not taken action to resolve the dispute. Here's a case where technology is ahead of the boots-on-the-ground forces. Clooney uses both the satellite technology and his role as a Hollywood celebrity to make the rest of the world aware of events affecting millions of people (in South Sudan as well as northern Sudan and now in Darfur).[29]

"Before-and-after satellite imagery indicated all of the tukuls *(mud huts) in the village of South Kordofan burned during recent April fighting. 'This [satellite] imagery provides independent confirmation of the devastating toll that the hostilities between the SRF and SAF continue to take on South Kordofan's civilian infrastructure,' the report states.*[30]

"Images taken of the Sudanese village of Abu Kershola on May 15, 2013 show 20 craters in residential and market areas. Analysts have opined that four were caused by artillery and the remaining 16 are consistent with aerial bombardment. 'This satellite imagery proves that armed forces remain

in at least 14 locations.... Sudan and South Sudan need to commit to complete compliance,' said Enough Project Sudan/South Sudan analyst Akshaya Kumar."[31]

The situation in South Sudan as well as Darfur still is fragile. With the peace contract agreed on by South Sudan and Sudan, some stability has occurred, despite the world's fear that things would unravel. Now there is growing tension and bombing in limited areas as a result of rebellions in Darfur and some areas not resolved in the CPA. But with new technologies such as the Sentinel Project offers, there will be major changes in how the rest of the world finds out about the areas most likely to experience widespread human suffering. The days of hiding the atrocities are now limited.

—៙—

Thirteen

Infrastructure

When I think of South Sudan and what it needs for the future, I have to reflect on the country I was born into, or at least the region of the White Nile River, where the Dinka are concentrated. A couple of years after my birth, a book was published entitled *Warriors of the White Nile: The Dinka*.[1] Ethnographer John Ryle and photographer Sarah Errington lived among the Dinka and they studied and photographed the people, detailing their customs, including cattle keeping, marriage negotiations, mothering, child raising, crop raising and many other aspects of their lives. They described the life and training of a warrior, who might look out for lions and hyena as well as Nuer trying to take some of their cattle. The two-story houses were featured, and effort went into describing the semi-nomadic life of moving from one area to the other depending on whether it was rainy season, when crops can be grown, or dry season, when only tobacco is grown in the temporary camp. The long walk to the river, six miles in the dry season, to collect water each day; the hair-dying customs among the men, using cattle urine; body decoration sessions—all these activities of the Dinka were detailed in a book that seemed to describe a kind of Eden still present in the early 1980s. The younger children especially wore few clothes, but T-shirts and draping gowns covered women and elders. The men's athleticism showed in the pictures depicting the thousands of Agar Dinka gathering for a communal spear-fishing event in the River Na'am at the end of the dry season.

The book was helpful in showing me how our life was before the civil war, as the conflict started a year after the book was published. In fact, it showed my father's village, now my mother's village, of Billing

Daldiar, so it was very near to my family's experiences before the bombing and attacks on Adut Maguen, just a short distance away. The big question is: what will it look like with the infrastructure—roads, dams, canals, electricity, water wells—that the country needs so badly. And how do we provide these in an orderly way so everyone feels they are getting their share.

I can also use Google Earth to pan over the South Sudan area where very few locations will spring up, as the villages are so small and the infrastructure—roads, schools, public buildings—is almost nonexistent. You will see after a while the vast expanse of the Sudd, the swamp around the White Nile around Shambe and the rivers flowing into it. You might pick up parts of the Jonglei Canal, now abandoned. You might see these, or you might not, because it is mostly a vast expanse of green. South Sudan is mostly rural villages with a few large towns and not a lot of cities. If you keep panning east toward Ethiopia, you might see the Akobo Desert, and the pictures of this will astound you. So South Sudan is an area just waiting for the right kinds of development. Jonglei Canal was stopped because, under the Sudanese government, it was felt not enough attention was paid to the changes in ways of life—especially farming in rainy season—that creating the canal would bring about.

Now with independence there will be great need for improvements in South Sudan, but they will probably come slowly, as that is our way. To go fast would upset the numerous tribal and other customs—ways people have been living for thousands of years. But the changes will come. It may seem like a small thing, but when I was growing up, land was tilled with single shovels and other basic tools. Now bulls are harnessed with plows to till the soil. The planting of crops goes faster. That is a big change.

Wells are being built in small numbers. There is still a problem with building them and maintaining them so that they will not fill in. One change is to build them with solid walls. These will hold the sides. Hand-pump wells, the most basic, are frequent in Rumbek, but not yet in the outlying areas. There are all kinds of ideas on how to build and power pumps, but we are better off with hand-pump wells distributed throughout our country rather than solar-powered wells in a couple of locations. Why? Everyone needs clean water, and if it is provided for one but not for others, there will be disruption and fighting over the well access.

It's a big problem that the rainy season in our area has changed. Sometimes it rains a lot, sometimes it doesn't. In 2009, there was a drought. It rained for the first months it normally does; it stopped in the middle, in June. That's not good because all the crops that they grow, if they are dry, it would be hard for them to grow back in the rainy season. So that is a really big problem. We need to see how to help them get water so they can have the crops that they grow.

So far, there are no wells in my home village, or in Stephen Chol Bayok's not too far from mine, or in any area around us. So that is what I hope to provide some day. Not having clean water makes life continue to be very harsh for our people.

There are no schools in our area. Two Lost Boys from Georgia and North Carolina have partnered with Mothering Across Continents, a North Carolina nonprofit organization, to build two schools in Unity State, north of our villages in our state. Those will not benefit anyone in Lakes State, but perhaps if we learn how to raise funds to build water wells, we can do the same to eventually build a school.

There are no clinics in our villages. If someone gets sick they have to carry them to the hospital in Rumbek. It's hard for somebody who cannot sit on the back of a bicycle, so it may go the old way of four people carrying the person. It takes them a while to carry a person the 12 miles to Rumbek. But once there, it's not a real hospital. There are no beds. Everyone lies on the floor. If you're in a room, it's hotter than staying outside. There is no place to send people, and it can get very full with children and everybody. It would be good to have a hospital just for children. You go there and get a prescription and then you have to go and buy the medicine outside the hospital—people go out and buy the medicine for the hospital. So if you don't have any money, nothing is going to happen.

However, small steady changes are coming with the money that flows to these areas from the United States due to the Lost Boys and other Sudanese sending money back. The villages are full of motorbikes. The last time I was there, some people would not even know how to ride a bike. Now there are lots of motorbikes.

Also, there are the satellite phones with generators. Generators also supply the lights within Rumbek. The generators they have in the villages to charge the phones are smaller than those generators. But the satellite-phone generators use pull cords, and they use gasoline. And there's a business that does this. You pay one Sudanese pound to have your battery charged.

With the motorbike I gave my brother, he can commute to Rumbek and leave his families in Billing Daldiar. That permits him to work and bring income from the water company where he works. My other brother, my younger brother, takes care of the family cattle, along with his children and his nieces and nephews. So there are some changes coming.

A big problem for South Sudan's infrastructure development is the delays or outright taking of the oil revenues from the oil wells that do exist in South Sudan. It was part of the CPA that these revenues would be divided equally, but there has been some trouble on this issue from Khartoum. Getting this problem solved quickly will be key to South Sudan's success. Then we will get to see the larger infrastructure changes.

—⚉—

The challenges facing the country are not unlike swimming under water—the task is so great it may not appear much progress is being made. At times it may seem like swimming against the tide as well. Creating schools, for instance, will require significant resources. In one state, Unity State, Mothering Across Continents (MAC) is working with several former Lost Boys as part of the Raising South Sudan project. With Mothering Across Continents support, one of these former Lost Boys, James Lubo Mijak from Charlotte, North Carolina, working with another Lost Boy, has completed construction of a permanent school building and teacher accommodations built to serve 300 children in his home village of Nyarweng. The other, Ngor Kur Mayol from Clarkston, Georgia, is in the planning stages for a school in his home village of Aliap. The two work on each other's schools to see them to completion. The projects include either building or reboring wells that have collapsed in order to provide community water, too. MAC provides fundraising help, operational back up and technical assistance, including working with well-drilling contractors and building contractors to make the projects a reality.

According to MAC Executive Director Patricia Shafer, in Unity State, there are 130 schools, but most of them are schools under a tree such as Majok described earlier in his refugee camp experience. Some have walls, but they are sheet metal and chicken wire, she said, and otherwise open to the elements. So the physical schools are not always available. The Nyarweng school her organization helped build is made of bricks and cement, and provides latrines as well. A teacher's living quarters, food storage, and teacher offices are also part of the model school in Nyarweng.

Schools in South Sudan are provided through a number of different sources: private schools, non-government organizations such as CARE International, and Mothering Across Continents. The government role in this will evolve as the country grows, but most organizations feel they cannot wait.[2]

Ngor Mayol was born in the small village of Aliap in Ruweng County in northern Unity State, near what is now the border with Sudan. Fighting broke out there, in 1983, near the critical line separating southern Sudan from the North, and he and thousands of other boys fled from the many villages around to go to the SPLA training camps, far away in Ethiopia. SPLA in the villages and towns escorted the boys to each succeeding town along the way until they reached a camp in Ethiopia, Tharapam. There they drilled in the camps in the morning and started learning their ABC's in classes in the afternoon, writing letters in the dirt with a stick.[3]

"They told us when the Northern militia comes, they kill boys," Ngor said. "When we went to the camp we trained, but we were not deployed. We were regularly screened and selected for more training." The younger boys were not part of the more intensive drilling, he said.

Several years later, in 1991, "We left Ethiopia; we were told we were going to Kenya for education, but it wasn't true." Eritrean rebels were fighting Ethiopia for independence, and Ethiopia had fallen, deposing John Garang's protector, Mengistu, and the SPLA camps had to move, just as Majok's camp at Pinyudo collapsed and emptied.

"We went to Kapoeta, and it was then when Riek Machar began fighting John Garang and splitting the SPLA. Those siding with Machar deserted the SPLA, so there were fewer soldiers to fight the war with northern Sudan."[4]

"John Garang had created the training camps to have soldiers when they became adults, but now he had to deploy them. I helped build a bunker for the assault on the Sudan Armed Forces landing field at Kapoeta," Ngor said. "These bunkers were made by digging a hole deep into the ground. The Northern Sudan bunkers were made of several layers of reinforcement—trees, dirt, steel roof—they could protect them from anything—except bombs. The SPLA bombed them with BOM30 long-range artillery and the bunkers were destroyed.[5]

"There were two rows of soldiers ringed around the inside of the circular bunker. I was in the second row. When the attack came, people died 10 feet from me. I was estimated to be 13 to 15 years old."

During the time Ngor was in the camps in Ethiopia, "John Garang came many times to talk to us.

"'You are the seed of South Sudan,'" he said. 'You are the engineers, the road builders, the teachers and more.' I was John Garang's bodyguard from 1994 to 1996. We people who knew him personally, it's something we will not forget. He was like George Washington to us."

Ngor said those in the training camps were allowed to leave periodically and go to school and then come back.

"The way it [training camps] were portrayed in Emma's War, *children abused and all, it was not like that. You were given a choice," Ngor said.*

While in the training camp in Kapoeta, Ngor and the others were told they were deploying to Bahr el Ghazal, but plans changed when one of the SPLA leaders who had rebelled against Garang returned to the SPLA. Later, in 1996, Ngor acquired travel documents and left and went south to Kenya, to Kakuma Refugee Camp, his first long-term opportunity for going to school and not being in the SPLA.

He found while at Kakuma that both his step-brothers had died in the war, on the same day, in 1990. When his father back in Aliap found out, he had a heart attack and died. His mother died the next year. He has surviving siblings, but has not located his younger brother, believed to be in Khartoum.

Part of the resettlement to Atlanta and Clarkston, Ngor attended high school in DeKalb County and began working for Publix Super Markets, Inc., where he's been employed for 10 years. In 2007, after his first return to southern Sudan in 2006, he and Karen Puckett founded the nonprofit Sudan Rowan, named for her home county in North Carolina. They associated with Mothering Across Continents on a project to build two schools in his home county, the one in the village of Nyarweng, Lubo's home, and a second in Aliap, Ngor's home.

Heavy on his mind is the elders' directive, "Don't forget your people," and Garang's "You are the seed of South Sudan," as well as the sacrifice of the lives of his four family members on account of the war. Ngor has worked both in Georgia, keeping his job with Publix, and in North Carolina, helping raise funds there, as well as in his Georgia home for building the schools. In the past year, he has worked as well in Ruweng County, in Unity State, while construction was under way on the first school.

"There were many challenges. The school was started when the border was open," but now because of both Sudan and South Sudan positioning themselves and engaging in attacks over the control of oil fields not too far away, the border has been closed, so materials could not be brought from the north. Fuel from contractors also became very expensive. But now materials are coming from Uganda (400 miles south) and a road, the first ever in the area, is being built. The UN is building a hard-surfaced road to connect two refugee camps, Yida and Ajuonthok. Yida is a major refugee camp for northern Sudanese from the Nuba Mountains. They fled from Southern

Kordofan state in Sudan because of attacks going on from the Bashir regime, continuing to kill its own people. Thousands are being cared for at Yida; there is also a school there, built by UNHCR.

Lubo and Ngor's school, Nyarweng Primary School, was started in 2011; the work slowed in 2012, and the school was constructed finally between February and May of 2013. The school actually began operation in 2012, occupying a building that was not quite finished. For a community that had no school previously, this was a small compromise to make. Finally, the Nyarweng Model School, the first of its kind, is open.

"There are two teachers paid by the state; three are volunteers. There were over 300 students, and they have moved back from Bentiu, the state capital, and other places in Payam district where they had to go to in order to have school," Ngor said, obviously proud of his and Lubo's work. "Mom and Dad can attend, too!"

The next phase, the school in Aliap, awaits more funding. Mothering Across Continents, Raising South Sudan from Atlanta, and Sudan Rowan will all be involved, as will other volunteers and contributors in the Atlanta and Charlotte communities and around the world.[6]

Fourteen

South Sudan's Future

What does South Sudan need, and what are its resources to achieve it? In the warm afterglow of independence, many ideas about the new nation and its future have emerged. Everyone is glad to be independent; after a 21-year war, and a six-year transition to independence, northern Sudan no long dictates all affairs in the world's newest country. Now, depending on who is speaking, it is the beginning of a bright new era, or a daunting task. It certainly is both. There are a great many needs, and a tremendous number of new opportunities.

The country is mostly composed of rural villages, with subsistence farming and cattle raising providing the economic activity, although cattle are rarely sold off, unless there are extreme weather conditions resulting in no grain.[1] As outlined in the discussion of John Garang's ideas of development for South Sudan, there are many approaches that can be utilized to create an economy based on the rural village and town model, but it will need to be done carefully. Looking at the country as it is, with large swaths of unadulterated land, some cultivated for crops and most for cattle grazing—it has to be remembered that there is no outright land ownership, but only a government-recognized right to use land.

Looking at the situation of South Sudan, with its eons-old traditions of a pastoralist society, now attempting to come of age and develop, next to a relatively advanced country, Sudan, it is possible to compare it to the point when European settlers first came to North America and found Native Americans. At that time, once depredations on either side occurred, the reaction was to conquer and destroy as a way of dealing with the intense differences in the societies. What if, instead of that approach, more advanced social

164

systems for cooperation were used to help bridge the wide differences in capacities for industry, agriculture, commerce and education? What if the conquering groups had done things differently then? What can be done now to help a similar transition among pastoralist communities in South Sudan as they face the challenges of the future?

Conflict within Sudan at the time of this writing, just past the second year of independence for South Sudan, is increasing. Salva Kiir, the president of the Government of South Sudan (GofSS), on July 22, 2013, dismissed a top vice president and former leader of a Civil War revolt against SPLM head John Garang, Riek Machar, and dissolved the government.[2] (Garang was Dinka; Kiir is Dinka; Machar is Nuer, the other largest ethnic group in South Sudan.) Meanwhile, articles in the Sudan Tribune *indicate peaceful efforts to resolve differences.[3]*

Then there are charges from the Sudan government that South Sudan's SPLA are supporting rebel groups in Darfur and in Blue Nile areas of Sudan where groups are organizing and fighting the Sudanese Army to bring about a secularized Sudan. That is the line that Khartoum is using to hold up the talks about dividing revenues from the only oil that either Sudan or South Sudan can currently pump, that lying in the disputed South Kordofan state. These oil fields, at Heglig (Arabic) or Panthou (Dinka) are actually in Ruweng County and are part of South Sudan. Abyei, an area nearby, does not yet have oil drilling, but has oil underground.[4] This area was to have its own referendum at the time of the South Sudan independence referendum in 2011, but mapping to define the referendum area was delayed over charges from the Sudan government that Misseriya tribesmen who grazed their livestock there should be included in the electorate. This objection has stopped implementation of referendum guidelines that had been agreed to after extensive mediated negotiations by Khartoum and the SPLM.[5]

The Key Issues: Oil and a Reformed Economy

All this points to the biggest, most important issue in South Sudan's economic life: the oil that lay in what was deemed southern Sudan lands was historically pumped north and the revenues supported development in northern Sudan. Now those revenues are needed for schools, government operations, security and the many other needs of a new government for a people totaling an estimated 8 million. But matters are at a stalemate as the

Bashir government halted the oil production in April of 2013 and, as of this writing, oil pumping was coming to a total stop.

Control of oil so that South Sudan could support itself was one of the main reasons for the Second Civil War. The Comprehensive Peace Agreement hammered out between Sudan and the SPLA after lengthy negotiations and signed in 2005 left the borders between the two countries subject to further discussions, and those talks have not resulted in a solution, as noted above. Without oil, the new country has no revenues. They have to resolve the issues of sharing revenues and the status of the lands themselves before World Bank loans or any other consistent form of funding government operations can be realized.

In the meantime, the efforts to educate young people, a hope of all who worked for conclusion of the war, is greatly affected by the stalemate. For the new model school that Lubo and Ngor worked on, there is the achievement of a large facility with four classrooms and housing for teachers to be proud of, together with a rebored well and latrines, offering a great improvement in village sanitation. This was paid for by individual donor and grant contributions to the Raising South Sudan project of MAC and partner nonprofit Sudan Rowan, based in Salisbury, North Carolina. Yet the teachers are still often volunteers. For a new school, the GofSS commits to pay the salary of the headmaster and at most one or two other teachers. As the government struggles to generate revenues, these are not the most secure incomes.[6]

Salaries are 300 South Sudanese pounds, or about $75 U.S. a month.[7] Numbers of people in the United States have raised the question, why don't the Lost Boys go back to South Sudan and help the country? In many cases, they have, but in others, the lack of infrastructure and jobs that will pay consistently and well keep them from doing this. They are able to send significant parts of their U.S. salaries back to South Sudan, and that has resulted in more cash being available in the local economy. Lost Boys pay for medical care and some of the conveniences mentioned in Majok's story of his family and his marriage and child. According to Mothering Across Continents Executive Director Patricia Shafer, there are project manager jobs available due to the building of a new pipeline from South Sudan to an Indian Ocean outlet either in Kenya or Ethiopia. Lubo, for instance, is employed in Unity State as a community development project manager by a Chinese oil firm.

But like much in South Sudan, things change rapidly from the original announced plans. Seeking to maintain job security, many Lost Boys stay on in the United States believing they can do more good for their families from overseas.[8]

Schools, water wells, clinics, scholarships to send South Sudanese students of promise to advanced education for the country's needs—all these are either delayed or just barely being provided in South Sudan today while the resolution of oil revenues disputes are being attempted. Still down the road are plans John Garang outlined and others have suggested to reform and improve the way farmers produce crops. Getting to a crop surplus situation where excess can become a major product for markets is still a way off. Creating a tourism industry that will take advantage of the wildlife in the vast areas of the countryside and the traditional ceremonial life in villages is still to come.

Key Issue: The Ability to Resolve Conflicts

Since the Rwandan and Somalian tragedies and since the end of apartheid in South Africa, the African Union has formed and taken an active role in trying to mediate disputes in countries on the continent. Likewise, the Union, which has developed a structure echoing that of the United Nations, with multiple functions to address a series of economic, political and emergency situations among the 54 member nations, has provided mediation help in the dispute between Sudan and South Sudan over the oilfields.

The oil pipeline moves oil from the wells at Heglig in Kordofan state, an area claimed by South Sudan, to the northern outlet to the sea, Port Sudan. In the Comprehensive Peace Agreement, the sharing of the well revenues was to be 50–50. Omar al–Bashir, president of Sudan, ordered the pipeline shut on June 8, 2013, because of hostile actions from local rebels. An article by Agence France-Press *in July 2013 said the two sides wanted even faster help than was being proposed for bringing the impasse to an end.*

"In a statement, Sudan and South Sudan confirm their acceptance of the AU plan and call on the African Union" and the prime minister of Ethiopia, chair of another regional body, "to put it into action immediately."[9]

Such steps presumably will be delayed as a result of South Sudan president Salva Kiir's dismissal of Riek Machar, the South Sudan representative in those talks. But Majok is optimistic that the changes will be accommodated. He says that more attention should be paid to the tribal disputes that feed the larger conflicts. (Intertribal conflicts have killed hundreds in Jonglei state since South Sudan's independence, according to the Sudan Tribune, *and the conflict is feeding the Sudan–South Sudan dispute over oil.)*[10]

Using Tribal Resources for Resolving Disputes

What happens is that they will shift people around, but the direction and the vision will not change. In terms of conflict management, there are some things that South Sudan can do that will resolve a lot of problems. Most of the conflicts arise on the local level, between groups raiding each others' cattle. This is a huge problem. When this happens, it's often part of a tribal rivalry, or it becomes more so because of the raid.

These people who are trying to reduce the conflict at the higher levels need to go to the people. There's a three-step way to bring these fights to an end:

1. Take the talks to the cattle camps. Meet with the leaders of the communities who have their cattle out in the bush, and talk with them to reduce the fights and raids between the communities.
2. Talk to the elders in the communities. These are the people whom other people listen to. They are looking at old age, and they don't get to participate in the community as they did when they were young. But they have a very large influence on the people in their community. Get their advice and have them give their counsel to the people who are fighting and raiding each other.
3. Those who are preaching conflict—work with them to stop that. There have always been those who were not happy—before the Civil War, during the Civil War, and now after. They need to stop preaching revenge and reprisal, and instead preach cooperation.

We need all the tribes in South Sudan to make this country work. The Sudan government loves to divide us and to set us against each other. But we need to stay together and work together. The conflict work needs to be done at the level where it starts—in the cattle camps and in the small villages.

Tribal councils come together to make what we Dinka term "the good decision." When conflicts arise or situations present themselves, the people, led by their chief and their elders, will sit in a circle to discuss what needs to be done. This is the traditional way, and it apparently has worked over many, many generations.

Ngor Mayol gave an example of this in a discussion of the increase in the price of cattle and the pressures to provide more cattle as bride-prices, especially since the Civil War. Bride-prices of 100 cows or more were being reported as common in some tribes in recent years; in past years such a price would have been an exception. The average price of a cow or bull has also increased dramatically.

"My tribe was affected by the war," Ngor said of the Dinka Pan-Aruu group he belongs to in northern Unity State. "Many people had been killed, families did not build their cattle herds—they lost a lot due to the war. So after the war, my tribe came together and said that a marriage, which used to cost 45 cows, should bring 25 cows. That should be the norm." In that way, the burden of creating bride-wealth could be reduced, and the high competitiveness that had come to mark it in some other communities could be avoided. This is a matter that was handled at the tribal level; the government does not get involved, Ngor said. If a marriage was to end in divorce—it does not happen very often—again the tribal court would make a judgment, awarding the groom only 25 cows even if he paid more, because this became the new custom among the Dinka Pan-Aruu.[11]

Counting Rich Resources, Developing Realistic Expectations

South Sudan has so many resources—oil that lies undiscovered, minerals we have yet to identify and find. The land offers a good climate, and little of the land is desert. We have the great expanse of the White Nile River. There are so many crops: sorghum, okra, millet, groundnuts (peanuts), casaba, sweet potatoes, tomatoes, melons, cabbage. Our trees give us kumquats, mangoes, shea butter and lemons. But building an economy based on these resources will take patience.

People in South Sudan need to know that South Sudan is not going to happen all at once. The first thing that we have to provide is water for our people—in the form of water wells. Providing water will help assure our crops can grow—that we will have food. Then we need to have schools and hospitals.

All these things will take time. It will take a while to be like other nations. We are moving in this direction, but it's going to take a while. If we try to have all that we think we need at once, we'll be disappointed. We have to be patient.

Other Countries Help to Raise a Country

South Sudan had a lot of help in coming to life from the countries on the same continent as well as from around the world. Its citizens and military suffered death and destruction and large-scale dislocation. As it gets on its way, it has help from a lot of individuals and countries as well.

The African Union, the union of 54 African states, has played a major role in encouraging resolution of differences between the two countries, particularly over the issue of oil, as noted above. As of this writing both countries were urging the assistance of the African Union in resolving the dispute.

The Union of South Africa has been very strong in support of South Sudan and in providing post-conflict reconstruction and development assistance in step with the African Union's focus on that nation-building capability. In 2011, it trained more than 1,600 officials from South Sudan's government in an effort to increase the abilities of the new nation to carry out government functions.[12] *According to Ngor, the police and security forces in South Sudan are being trained by South African government police officials.*

The United States has been spurred by the many efforts of individuals like the late Mickey Leland, the congressman from Texas who died in a 1989 plane crash on a mountain slope in Ethiopia while trying to bring to light the massive starvation and desperate conditions at Pinyudo and other refugee camps; NBA player Manute Bol bringing food to Pachala; George Clooney focusing international attention on the eve of the referendum vote; and the thousands of news items that came out of the Lost Boys' stories as they arrived in the United States as well as Canada and Australia. Whole communities across the United States took the Boys into their homes, schools, and businesses. Many churches have become involved, and several nonprofits have been created to assist those back in South Sudan. Now men (and women, as those brought into foster care in the United States included girls), the Boys continue to educate anyone they can about the atrocities that occurred.

In addition, there are many South Sudanese in the diaspora, people who escaped to Egypt, the Middle East, the United States, Canada, and Australia, who watch U.S. and other countries' support of South Sudan as it continues its efforts to survive despite efforts of Sudan to circumvent the Comprehensive Peace Agreement.

The Obama administration's then–U.S. ambassador to the United Nations, Susan Rice, told NPR after the referendum in 2011 that the United

States regards Sudan as a state sponsor of terrorism, and that it will only consider lifting sanctions against the country if they abide by the CPA. She said the issue goes "back to 1993, when it was necessary for us to put Sudan on the state sponsors of terrorism lists, as they were housing and harboring Osama bin Laden and supporting many other terrorist organizations at the time. And then there have been subsequent sanctions, both imposed legislatively and by the executive branch.

"In our discussions with the government of Sudan, we laid out ... a very detailed road map for how we could work to improve our bilateral relationship in a step-by-step fashion, in accordance with actions taken by the government, and actions that would be reciprocated by us. The first step in that process was to see the successful conclusion of the Comprehensive Peace Agreement. A crucial element of that was, of course, the referendum."

Now, she said, things depend on the status of Abyei. "Rather than dealing with it at the negotiating table, the government moved forces into Abyei and continue to occupy it—since May [now withdrawn]. There is the issue of revenue-sharing and oil. There's the issue of the disputed border areas. There's the issue of ensuring that citizens of the North and the South have certain rights that are respected and ensured in their respective countries. All of these are formal parts of the Comprehensive Peace Agreement, as is the status of Blue Nile and Southern Kordofan, where fighting is raging. So these are all issues that we can't sweep under the rug and pretend are not part of the CPA."[13]

In addition to the interest of the United States, Canada, and Australia, there is interest in South Sudan from many other countries. China, which built the oil pipeline from Heglig (Panthou) to the North's Port Sudan and developed the port itself, is keen to see the oil flow; India and Malaysia are partners in the enterprise. Japan's Toyota has told South Sudan it wants to help develop a new pipeline that will bypass Sudan and access the Indian Ocean through Kenya, a very attractive prospect to South Sudan.[14]

So South Sudan, the world's newest country, carved out of the largest country in Africa, home of the White Nile River and the world's largest swamp, and holder of oil and other unknown mineral resources as well as a climate ideal for many agricultural crops, has many challenges, and many opportunities ahead of it.

Fifteen

Warriors in a
Different Kind of War

In the Second Civil War, the one that chased me from my home, it is estimated that 2 million people in southern Sudan died and 4 million were displaced.[1] This was the second war since British rule ended in 1956. In that first war, the one my grandmother referred to when she warned me about war coming again, many also died.

The Dinka are not afraid of war, but there needs to be a different kind of war, one that uses our other gifts—the ability to meet together and discuss and find solutions that are more peaceful. In our journey to Ethiopia we were always conscious that an unintended action could affect us—someone could get mad, someone could easily harm us. In fact, the people who were most helpful to us as we journeyed were the women and the old people. Those men of fighting age remained silent and did not help us when we needed directions or food or other things. There are tribes within South Sudan that still have difficulty getting along with each other. Competition over cattle-grazing lands and water are big areas of disagreement.

So the threat of conflict is always there. But we need to do better than that. We need to see ourselves in South Sudan as warriors in a new war—a war to bring ourselves up to the modern age in terms of infrastructure. We need to arm ourselves with new tools and new weapons. Chief among these is education. We need to build wells for water, roads for access, and we need to build schools and clinics.

This emphasis on education goes against the old tradition among the Dinka and possibly other tribes. In fact, education was associated with schools, and schools were associated with towns, as only towns had enough people to attract students from the surrounding areas. For instance, I was designated to receive schooling, and the school was in another town, where I would go to live. When we were part of the former Sudan, everything would have been in Arabic, and only one son would be educated.

In the old days before the SPLA, the Dinka did not trust the towns. Towns were where people learned non–Dinka ways. A boy might become subject to the attractions of the town and get involved in crime or drink, spoiling him for life as a Dinka cattle keeper. So the Dinka mistrusted schools, and the boy who was selected to be educated was one who was not so good at cattle keeping and other traditional duties of a Dinka male.

Towns, too, were places where raids had occurred in the past when Arabs from the north invaded and took away children and girls, enslaving them over time. While this happened mostly to the Malual Dinka, in the northern Bahr el Ghazal area, it was still a threat to other Dinka, including the Agar Dinka. So opposed were the Agar Dinka to engaging with towns and outside cultures that they discouraged roads being built to their areas. Isolation was seen as a good thing. Between lack of access to their grazing lands and the Agar Dinka's reputation as fierce warriors, the people remained relatively undisturbed by the hand of civilization.

Now, since the 1980s, the Dinka attitude toward education has changed. People saw during the civil war that the soldiers who had positions of authority in the SPLA were like their leader, John Garang—educated. John Garang himself had been educated in Iowa, at Grinnell College and at Iowa State University, where he received a Ph.D.

He spoke like a professor, but very clearly, and always emphasized reading and learning for all he spoke to. Our people quickly grasped the connection between being literate and gaining their freedom from domination by other groups.

The attitudes toward engagement with the outside world have also changed. We now favor roads that can make it easier to get to clinics. We want the water service and the telephone service and easier transportation so that we can get to other communities to be with relatives and to enhance our villages.

So the Dinka now embrace education and engagement, although our traditions are still intact otherwise. These values include: respect for other tribes, care for our cattle, care for our families, consulting with each other in times of difficulty to reach agreement, high regard for elders, and the value of celebration—carrying on the intricate rites of dance and song and body decoration.

Standing Up for Refugees

I hope through this book to speak for the many refugees who remain in Kakuma and other refugee camps in Africa. While many Sudanese have left to return to their new country, there are many more taking their places from other conflicts and unstable areas; some remain from Sudan, others from Rwanda, and from Somalia as well as other areas experiencing crisis. In Syria, as I write this, more refugees are being created from the protracted war there. All of them share a common problem: They want to have a home, but they cannot go home. And conditions in the camps are never easy.

We Lost Boys are the people who passed through different life experiences, cultures, weather, and languages. It is hard for any one of the Lost Boys not to communicate well because we acquired languages in order to survive. My dream is to make some people's lives better through my book. I want readers to recognize the difficulties of children in refugee camps. I want refugee children around the world to know that Majok Marier from the Lost Boys of Sudan is standing up for you. I do know how hard it is in the refugee camps; I was there not so many years ago. I know it is not simple to be in the refugees' situation. I hope my ideas will support many thousands of refugees right now around the world. I will encourage you to hope for the best in any difficult situation you are now in. I was a witness to people dying, young children dying, because they could not bear the thought of not having food they expected to have. You have to keep hope for the better, for a changed future sometime later in your life. I want you not to lose hope completely in your dreams.

I am glad to have passed through this difficult situation of killing, starvation, thirst, and going without parents. I want my book to make change for everyone who has some issue in his or her life. For this person, I say this: I need you to make yourself like the Lost Boys of Sudan to be successful in your life. The Lost Boys are people who have long been patient regarding the difficulties they face in life. We are lacking many things in our lives still, but we are proud, and we are going on with our planning for our changed life every day. I love being a Lost Boy of Sudan, to have made this tough change in my lifetime, and to have survived. And

I think my experiences can help some people to have the presence of mind to deal with any situation they are living in now.

I hope every person reading this book now can have knowledge of at least this African country. There are many others, each with its own unique history and events to appreciate. I hope you can understand the difficulties that arose over our history. Sudan, a country that killed her own citizens every year, never fought any different nation in her history. The wars were waged on her own people, and the two civil wars that have resulted come from the native peoples' refusal to be bound by the stupidity of the government's leaders.

A Call for African Unity

While I spent nine years in Kenya in Kakuma Refugee Camp, I remember the beatings by the Kenyan police, the long lines for food desperately needed, and the attacks of the Turkana tribesmen that killed our residents. There were other mistreatments by our own southern Sudanese and Ethiopians as well. These were attacks on Africans by Africans. Kenya did not remember that we were African brothers, sisters, and neighboring country people. I do not blame its citizens so much, but leaders who did not set better rules for people to respect one another as the neighbors they were. Africans lack unity, forgiveness, support and the independence to solve their own problems. African leaders tend to love for outside people to solve their illegal affairs even though they are responsible for creating the problems. So how long are other people going to solve their problems? I am now ending up here in America where my life is based on paying confusing bills every day—far from my home country, not being as productive as I could for my country—as a result of these wars. This conflict needs to stop.

Africa is a beautiful continent that is full of the best animals, oil, gold, diamonds, and open land. It is a center of many great foods and fruits of the world. She is created in the image of God, a beautiful continent with more than most areas of the world. We as Africans all abuse our beautiful land badly because of the war and conflict from our political parties. Africa is a center of war and diseases that are not cured, and our leaders are not ashamed of the number of Africans dying because of these. Most people look forward to visiting Africa to see beautiful animals they don't have in their own countries. But our leaders do not take advantage of this opportunity to develop their countries. It is discouraging for African citizens to cry for help every year in their own home. This is a painful thing in my life as an African man in this world. I want African leaders to have dialogues and talks to save another generation, which is coming up now.

I believe one day African people can come together to build a united Africa. We are crying for a whole Africa free of many things like AIDS, wars, starvation, corruption, and poor economics. We need clean water, schools conducive to learning, and clinics in our rural villages. I hope African leaders will think about people's future, if my book can reach them. African leaders, you need to make some changes. Please—many people are leaving countries because of wars. Many countries are falling apart all over the continent. Leaders from all of these regions should sit down and discuss African affairs in general to save its citizens.

Final Thoughts

I remember my home in Adut Maguen before I fled to Ethiopia. I was just a young boy then, but watched the cattle and engaged in games with others doing the same. I played with my cousin, Kolnyin Nak Goljok, and several other boys and girls. We played at night in traditional dancing circles. Just as I missed my family, my brothers, sister, mother and grandmother during my long journey, I missed playing with these children. I remember the grasses that were so tall and green during the rainy season. I didn't get to have the many fruits that grew in our village and that I loved to eat all the time.

I missed out growing up with these children, and around my village people who were so full of love. The people in my village always supported each other, and I grew up without knowing these people, for I was away. I missed the rites of manhood, when I would become a *parapuol*, as my brothers did, with the scars to show my bravery.

My hope for my daughter Adikdik and for future children I may have and all the children in Africa is that the war that visited me will never find them. I will do all in my power to make sure that hers—and theirs—is as peaceful a life as possible. We owe this to those we lost on our long journey. May their lives count for this—that more peace than war will come to this bountiful land of Africa, especially the region of the Sudd, South Sudan.

Appendix: Aid Groups in Ethiopia and Kenya

Aid Groups in Pinyudo Refugee Camp, Ethiopia

United Nations High Commissioner for Refugees (UNHCR)
World Food Program
International Red Cross
Médecins Sans Frontières (MSF; Doctors Without Borders)
United Nations Children's Fund (UNICEF)
Radda Barnen (Save the Children Foundation)

Aid Groups in Kakuma Refugee Camp, Kenya

United Nations High Commissioner for Refugees (UNHCR)
World Vision
International Red Cross
Médecins Sans Frontières (MSF; Doctors Without Borders)
Lutheran World Federation
International Organization for Migrants (IOM)

Notes

Chapter One

1. John Ryle and the editors of Time-Life Books, *Warriors of the White Nile: The Dinka* (Amsterdam: Time-Life Books, 1982), 25.

2. Marjorie M. Fisher et al., eds., *Ancient Nubia: African Kingdoms on the Nile* (Cairo: American University in Cairo Press, 2012), 10.

3. Grzmski Krzstzof, *American Visions* 8, no. 5 (Oct./Nov. 1993), 7–8.

4. Ibrahim M. Omer, "Nubia: Religion: Anubis," Ancient Sudan~Nubia, http://www.ancientsudan.org/religion_05_anubis.html (accessed May 15, 2013).

5. Ibrahim M. Omer, "Nubia: Religion: Isis," Ancient Sudan~Nubia website, http://www.ancientsudan.org/religion_03_isis.html, accessed May 15, 2013.

6. Fisher, *Ancient Nubia*, 26.

7. Joseph O. Vogel, ed., "Egypt and Sub-Saharan Africa: Their Interaction," *Encyclopedia of Precolonial Africa* (Walnut Creek, CA: AltaMira Press, 1997), 465–472. http://www.wysinger.homestead.com/su-saharan.html (accessed April 21, 2013).

8. "Mohammad Ali," *Gale Encyclopedia of Biography*, http://www.answers.com/topic/muhammad-ali (accessed July 20, 2013).

9. Fisher, *Ancient Nubia*, 40–42.

10. "History of the Sudan: Nubia: from 3000 BC," *History World.net*, from 2001, on-going. http://www.historyworld.net/wrldhis/PlainTextHistories.asp?historyid=aa86 (accessed December 26, 2013).

11. Ryle, *White Nile*, 24.

12. Ibid., 24–28; "Mohammad Ali."

13. Ryle, *White Nile*, 28

14. *Encyclopaedia Britannica*, "Sudan: The Growth of National Consciousness." http://www.britannica.com/EBchecked/topic/571417/Sudan/24319/The-growth-of-national-consciousness (accessed May 18, 2013).

15. Fisher, *Ancient Nubia*, 40–42.

16. "Sudan: National Consciousness."

17. Ryle, *White Nile*, 25.

18. "South Sudan Backs Independence-Results," BBC News. Feb. 7, 2011. http://www.bbc.co.uk/news/world-africa-12379431, (accessed May 18, 2013).

Chapter Five

1. "Lost Boys of Sudan: 12 Years Later," CBS News, *60 Minutes*, March 31, 2013, http://www.cbsnews.com/3102-18560_162-57576821.html.

Chapter Eight

1. Deborah Scroggins, *Emma's War* (New York: Vintage, 2004), 256–80.

Chapter Nine

1. "Africa Millions Dead in Sudan Civil War," BBC News, December 11, 1998, http://www.news.bbc.co.uk/2/hi/africa/232803.stm.
2. Julie Flint, "The Return of a Sudanese Survivor," *Daily Star*, July 19, 2005, http://www.dailystar.com.lb/Opinion/Commentary/Jul/19/The-return-of-a-Sudanese-survivor.ashx#axzz2T2TwPOIK.
3. Ibid.
4. Deborah Scroggins, *Emma's War*, 263, 274–279.
5. John Garang in interview with Scott Simon, National Public Radio, *Weekend Edition*, February 11, 2005, http://www.npr.org/templates/story/story.php?storyId=4496451.
6. Ibid.
7. "New VP Enters Evolving Sudanese Government," UPI.com, August 14, 2005, http://www.upi.com/Top_News/2005/08/14/New-VP-enters-evolving-Sudan-government/UPI-75091124030107/.
8. Ibid.

Chapter Twelve

1. "Manute Bol: 1985–1995, Career Statistics," *NBAwww*, http://www.nba.com/historical/playerfile/index.html?player=manute_bol (accessed June 29, 2013); Phil Jasner, "Remembering the Best of Times with Former NBA Player Manute Bol," *Philadelphia Inquirer*, http://articles.philly.com/2010-06-21/sports/24965043_1_don-feeley-dinka-tribesman-manute-bol (accessed June 19, 2013).
2. Jasner.
3. Ibid.
4. Ibid.
5. Alan Sharavsky, "Manute Bol: NBA Player Who Cared," *Philadelphia Inquirer*, July 13, 2004. http://articles.philly.com/2004-07-13/news/25372629_1_sudan-famine-manute-bolsudanese; Keith Pompey, "Former Sixer Manute Bol Dead at 47," *Philadelphia Inquirer*, June 19, 2010, http://articles.philly.com/2010-06-19/news/24962641_1_bol-first-sudan-sunrise-manute-bol.
6. Jasner.
7. "Manute Bol Remembered as 'Also a Giant off the Court' at Funeral," *USA Today*, http://usatoday30.usatoday.com/sports/basketball/nba/2010-06-29-manute-bol-funeral_N.htm (accessed June 26, 2013).
8. "Manute Bol Remembered"; El Tayeb Siddig, "Basketball Star Bol Buried in South Sudan," Reuters, July 4, 2010, http://www.reuters.com/assets/print?aid=USTRE663K320100704.
9. Siddig, "Bol Buried."
10. William A. Martin, "Ohlone's Standing Slam Dunk," Ohlone College, http://www.ohlone.edu/org/athletics/mensbasketball/teamnews20082009/20080925ohlonesslamdunk.html (accessed July 14, 2013).
11. "Model Profile: Alek Wek," *New York Magazine* "Fashion News," http://nymag.com/fashion/models/awek/alekwek (accessed June 26, 2013); "Alek Wek Profile," *Hello!*, http://www.hellomagazine.com/profiles/alek-wek/ (accessed June 26, 2013).
12. "Alek Wek Profile."
13. "Model Profile: Alek Wek"; "Alek Wek," UNHCR: Against All Odds, http://www.playagainstallodds.com/factualweb/us/2.3/articles/alek_wek.html (accessed June 27, 2013).
14. "Author Bios," They Poured Fire on Us from the Sky, http://www.theypouredfire.com/authors.htm (accessed Aug. 5, 2013).
15. Ibid.
16. "Biography for Ger Duany," IMDB.com, November 2004, http://www.imdb.com/name/nm1563346/bio (accessed June 28, 2013); Tambay A. Obenson, "Arnold Oceng, Ger Duany, Emmanuel Jal Will Play 'Lost Boys' in America in 'The Good Lie,'" Indiewire.com, http://blogs.indiewire.com/shadowandact/arnold-oceng-ger-duany-emmanuel-jal-will-play-lost-boys-in-america-in-the-good-lie (accessed June 28, 2013); Obenson.
17. John Avlon, "A 21st Century Statesman," *Newsweek*, February 28, 2011, cover, 16–23.
18. Ibid.
19. Ibid.
20. "Our Mission," *The Enough Project*, http://www.enoughproject.org/about (accessed July 14, 2013).
21. Avlon.
22. Ibid.
23. Ibid.
24. Ibid.
25. Ibid.

26. "George Clooney's Satellite Sentinel Project Reveals War Crimes, Security Violations Using DigitalGlobe Imagery," Satellite Today.com, June 17, 2013, http://www.satellitetoday.com/st/feature/George-Clooneys-Satellite-Sentinel-Project-Reveals-War-Crimes-Security-Violations-Using-Digital Globe-Imagery_41401.html.

27. Steve Paterno, "Sudan Rebel Leader on Limelight While President in Panic," *Sudan Tribune*, July 17, 2008, http://www.sudan tribune.com/spip.php?article27906.

28. "Clooney's Satellite."

29. Ibid.

30. Ibid.

31. Ibid.

Chapter Thirteen

1. Ryle, *Warriors of the White Nile: The Dinka*.

2. Patricia Shafer, email to Estelle Ford-Williamson, July 29, 2013.

3. Ngor Kur Mayol, interview, Estelle Ford-Williamson, July 13, 2013.

4. Ibid.

5. Ngor Kur Mayol, interview, Estelle Ford-Williamson, July 21, 2013.

6. Ibid.

Chapter Fourteen

1. S.J. Dima, "Land Use Systems in South Sudan and Their Impacts on Land Degradation: A Paper Presented at the Conference on Environmental Management Plan in Post Conflict South Sudan," http://free pdfdb.org/doc/land-use-systems-in-south-sudan-and-their-impacts-on-land-11248962.html (accessed July 23, 2013).

2. "South Sudan's Kiir Relieves VP Machar and Dissolves Government," *Sudan Tribune*. July 22, 2013. http://www.sudan tribune.com/spip.php?iframe&page=imprimable&id_article=47380.

3. "South Sudan Denies Division over Potential Candidate for Vice-President Post,"

The Sudan Tribune, July 27, 2013. http://www.sudantribune.com/spip.php?article 47431.

4. Ngor Kur Mayol, conversation with Estelle Ford-Williamson, July 29, 2013.

5. "Sudan's NCP says SPLM has three options to resolve impasse over Abyei," *Sudan Tribune*, November 9, 2010. http://www.sudantribune.com/spip.php?article36884.

6. Patricia Shafer, email to Estelle Ford-Williamson, July 29, 2013.

7. Ngor Kur Mayol, interview with Estelle Ford-Williamson, July 13, 2013.

8. Shafer, July 29, 2013.

9. "Two Sudans Want Faster African Solution to Oil Row," *Agence France-Presse*, July 1, 2013, http://www.globalpost.com/dispatch/news/afp/130701/two-sudans-want-faster-african-solution-oil-row.

10. Tesfa-Alem Tekle, "Thousands of Refugees Flee Conflict in S. Sudan's Jonglei State, Says UN," *Sudan Tribune*, July 22, 2013, http://www.sudantribune.com/spip.php?article47359.

11. Ngor Kur Mayol, interview with the authors, July 21, 2013.

12. "South Africa, South Sudan Establish Ties," South African Government News Agency, September 27, 2011, http://south-africa.info/news/international/southsudan-270911.htm.

13. Susan Rice, "The Path Ahead for South Sudan," interview with Neal Conan, NPR Talk of the Nation, July 11, 2011, http://www.npr.org/2011/07/11/137770066/the-path-ahead-for-south-sudan.

14. Jeremy Taylor, "Oil Politics, Asian Suitors, and Alternative Pipelines in South Sudan," *Think Africa Press*, June 26, 2013, http://thinkafricapress.com/south-sudan/oil-politics-asian-suitors-alternative-pipelines-south-sudan.

Chapter Fifteen

1. "Millions Dead in Sudan Civil War," BBC News, December 11, 1998, http://news.bbc.co.uk/2/hi/africa/232803.stm.

Bibliography

Ajak, Benjamin, Alphonsian Deng, Benson Deng, and Judy Bernstein. *They Poured Fire on Us from the Sky*. New York: Public Affairs, 2006.

"Alek Wek." *UNHCR: Against All Odds* online game. http://www.playagainstallodds.com/factualweb/us/2.3/articles/alek_wek.html.Accessed June 27, 2013.

"Alek Wek Profile." *HELLO!* Online TV Magazine. http://www.hellomagazine.com/profiles/alek-wek/. Accessed June 26, 2013.

"Author Bios." *They Poured Fire on Us from the Sky*. http://www.theypouredfire.com/authors.htm. Accessed August 5, 2013.

Avlon, John. "A 21st Century Statesman." *Newsweek*, February 28, 2011, Cover, 16–23.

Beckwith, Carol, and Angela Fisher. "Dinka: Legendary Cattle Keepers of Sudan." National Geographic Society illustrated lecture based on NGS book by same title. http://www.youtube.com/watch?v=erNAdYoqaFo. Accessed August 6, 2013.

"Biography for Ger Duany." IMDBwww. Posted November, 2004. http://www.imdb.com/name/nm1563346/bio. Accessed June 28, 2013.

Bixler, Mark. *The Lost Boys of Sudan*. Athens: University of Georgia Press, 2006.

Dau, Jon Bull, and Michael S. Sweeney. *God Grew Tired of Us*. Washington, D.C.: National Geographic Society, 2007.

Dima, S.J. "Land Use Systems in South Sudan and Their Impacts on Land Degradation: A Paper Presented at the Conference on Environmental Management Plan in Post Conflict South Sudan." http://freepdfdb.org/doc/land-use-systems-in-south-sudan-and-their-impacts-on-land-11248962.html. Accessed July 23, 2013.

Eggers, Dave. *What Is the What?* New York: Vintage, 2007.

Encyclopaedia Britannica. "Sudan: The Growth of National Consciousness." http://www.britannica.com/EBchecked/topic/571417/Sudan/24319/The-growth-of-national-consciousness. Accessed May 18, 2013.

Fisher, Marjorie M., Peter Lacovara, Salima Ikram, and Sue D'Auria, eds. *Ancient Nubia: African Kingdoms on the Nile*. Cairo: American University in Cairo Press, 2012.

Flint, Julie. "The Return of a Sudanese Survivor." *Daily Star*, July 19, 2005. http://www.dailystar.com.lb/Opinion/Commentary/Jul/19/The-return-of-a-Sudanese-survivor.ashx#axzz2T2TwPOIK.

Garang, John. Interview by Scott Simon. *Weekend Edition*, NPR, February 11, 2005. http://www.npr.org/templates/story/story.php?storyId=4496451.

Hughes, Dana. "George Clooney Arrested at Sudanese Embassy." ABC News. March 16, 2012. http://abcnews.go.com/Politics/OTUS/george-clooney-arrested-sudan-embassy-washington-dc/story?id=15936415.

International Committee for the Red Cross. http://www.icrc.org/eng/index.jsp.

International Organization for Migrants. http://www.iom.int.

Jasner, Phil. "Remembering the Best of Times with Former NBA Player Manute Bol." http://articles.philly.com/2010-06-21/sports/24965043_1_don-feeley-dinka-tribesman-manute-bol. Accessed June 19, 2013.

Jok, Jok Madut. *Sudan: Race, Religion, and Violence*. Oxford: One World, 2009.

Krzstzof, Grzmski. "Nubia." *American Visions*, 8, no. 5 (October/November 1993), 7–8.

"Lost Boys of Sudan: 12 Years Later." *60 Minutes*, CBS News, March 31, 2013. http://www.www.cbsnews.com/3102-18560_162-57576821.html.

Lutheran World Federation. http://www.lutheranworld.org/.

"Manute Bol: 1985–1995, Career Statistics." NBA.com. http://www.nba.com/historical/playerfile/index.html?player=manute_bol. Accessed June 29, 2013.

"Manute Bol Remembered as 'Also a Giant Off the Court" at Funeral." *USA Today*. http://usatoday30.usatoday.com/sports/basketball/nba/2020-06-29-manute-bol-funeral_N.htm. Accessed June 26, 2013.

Martin, William A. "Ohlone's Standing Slam Dunk." Ohlone College. http://www.ohlone.edu/org/athletics/mensbasketball/teamnews20082009/20080925ohlones slamdunk.html. Accessed July 14, 2013.

Mayol, Ngor Kur. Interview with Estelle Ford-Williamson, July 13, 2013.

_____. Interview with Estelle Ford-Williamson, July 21, 2013.

_____. Interview with Estelle Ford-Williamson, July 29, 2013.

_____. Interview with the authors, July 21, 2013.

Médecins Sans Frontières (Doctors Without Borders). http://www.msf.org.

"Millions Dead in Sudan Civil War." BBC News, December 11, 1998. http://www.news.bbc.co.uk/2/hi/africa /232803.stm.

"Model Profile: Alek Wek." *New York* "Fashion News." http://nymag.com/fashion/models/awek/alekwek. Accessed June 26, 2013.

Mothering Across Continents. http://motheringacrosscontinents.org/RaisingSouth Sudan/.

"Muhammad Ali." *Gale Encyclopedia of Biography*. http://www.answers.com/topic/muhammad-ali. Accessed July 20, 2013.

"New VP Enters Evolving Sudanese Government." UPI.com. August 14, 2005. http://www.upi.com/Top_News/2005/08/14/New-VP-enters-evolving-Sudan-government/UPI-75091124030107/.

Obenson, Tambay A. "Arnold Oceng, Ger Duany, Emmanuel Jal Will Play 'Lost Boys' in America in 'The Good Lie.'" Indiewirewww.http://blogs.indiewire.com/shadow andact/arnold-oceng-ger-duany-emmanuel-jal-will-play-lost-boys-in-america-in-the-good-lie. Accessed June 28, 2013.

Omer, Ibrahim M. "Nubia: Religion: Anubis." Ancient Sudan~Nubia. http://www.ancientsudan.org/religion_05_anubis.html. Accessed May 15, 2013.

_____. "Nubia: Religion: Isis." Ancient Sudan~Nubia. http://www.ancientsudan.org/religion_03_isis.html. Accessed May 15, 2013.

"Our Mission." The Enough Project. http://www.enoughproject.org/about. Accessed July 14, 2013.

Paterno, Steve. "Sudan Rebel Leader on Limelight While President in Panic." *Sudan Tribune*. July 17, 2008. http://www.sudantribune.com/spip.php?article27906.

Pompey, Keith. "Former Sixer Manute Bol Dead at 47." June 19, 2010. *Philadelphia Inquirer*. http://articles.philly.com/2010-06-9/news/24962641_1_bol-first-sudan-sunrise-manute-bol.

Radda Barnen (Save the Children). http://www.savethechildren.se/.

Rice, Susan. "The Path Ahead for South Sudan." Interview with Neal Conan. *Talk of the Nation*, NPR. July 11, 2011. http://www.npr.org/2011/07/11/137770066/the-path-ahead-for-south-sudan.

Ryle, John, and the Editors of Time-Life Books. *Warriors of the White Nile: The Dinka*. Amsterdam: Time-Life Books, 1982.

St. John, Warren. *Outcasts United*. New York: Spiegel & Grau, 2009.

Schuster, Steve. "George Clooney's Satellite Sentinel Project Reveals War Crimes, Security Violations Using DigitalGlobe Imagery." *Satellite Today.com*. June 17, 2013. http://www.satellitetoday.com/st/feature/George-Clooneys-Satellite-Sentinel-Project-Reveals-War-Crimes-Security-Violations-Using-DigitalGlobe-Imagery_41401.html.

Scroggins, Deborah. *Emma's War*. New York: Vintage, 2004.

Shafer, Patricia. Email to Estelle Ford-Williamson, July 29, 2013.

Siddig, El Tayeb. "Basketball Star Bol Buried in South Sudan." Reuters, July 4, 2010. http://www.reuters.com/assets/print?aid=USTRE663K320100704.

"South Africa, South Sudan Establish Ties." South African Government News Agency, September 27, 2011. http://southafrica.info/news/international/southsudan-270911.htm.

"South Sudan Backs Independence-Results." BBC News, February 7, 2011. http://www.bbc.co.uk/news/world-africa-12379431.

"South Sudan Denies Division over Potential Candidate for Vice-President Post." *Sudan Tribune*, July 27, 2013. http://www.sudantribune.com/spip.php?article47431.

"South Sudan's Kiir Relieves VP Machar and Dissolves Government." *Sudan Tribune*, July 22, 2013. http://www.sudantribune.com/spip.php?iframe&page=imprimable&id_artil=47380.

"Sudan's NCP says SPLM has three options to resolve impasse over Abyei." *Sudan Tribune*, November 9, 2010. http://www.sudantribune.com/spip.php?article36884.

Taylor, Jeremy. "Oil Politics, Asian Suitors, and Alternative Pipelines in South Sudan." *Think Africa Press*, June 26, 2013. http://thinkafricapress.com/south-sudan/oil-politics-asian-suitors-alternative-pipelines-south-sudan.

Tekle, Tesfa-Alem. "Thousands of Refugees Flee Conflict in S. Sudan's Jonglei State, Says UN." *Sudan Tribune*, July 22, 2013. http://www.sudantribune.com/spip.php?article47359.

"Two Sudans Want Faster African Solution to Oil Row." *Agence France-Presse*, July 1, 2013. http://www.globalpost.com/dispatch/news/afp/130701/two-sudans-want-faster-african-solution-oil-row.

United Nations Children's Fund (UNICEF). http://www.unicef.org/.

United Nations High Commissioner for Refugees (UNHCR). http://www.unhcr.org/.

World Food Programme. http://www.wfp.org/.

World Vision. http://www.worldvision.org.

Index

Numbers in **_bold italics_** indicate pages with photographs.